SURFING THE MENU

SURFING THE MENU

Two chefs, one journey: a fresh-food adventure

Ben O'Donoghue AND Curtis Stone

Photographs by Ben Dearnley, Craig Kinder and Ewan Robinson

KEY PORTER BOOKS

FOR CAROLYN FOULNER

First published in 2008 in Canada and the United States by Key Porter Books Limited.
First published in Australia by ABC Books for the
AUSTRALIAN BROADCASTING CORPORATION
GPO Box 9994 Sydney 2001
Australia

Library and Archives Canada Cataloguing in Publication

Stone, Curtis
    Surfing the menu / Curtis Stone and Ben O'Donoghue.

ISBN 978-1-55470-082-0 (bound)

    1. Cookery, Australian. I. O'Donoghue, Ben II. O'Donoghue, Ben.
Surfing the menu. III. Title.
TX725.A8S76 2008   641.5994   C2008-901447-2

The publisher gratefully acknowledges the support of the Canada Council for the Arts and the Ontario Arts Council
for its publishing program. We acknowledge the support of the Government of Ontario through the Ontario Media
Development Corporation's Ontario Book Initiative.

We acknowledge the financial support of the Government of Canada through the Book Publishing Industry
Development Program (BPIDP) for our publishing activities.

Key Porter Books Limited
Six Adelaide Street East, Tenth Floor
Toronto, Ontario
Canada M5C 1H6

www.keyporter.com

Printed and bound in Singapore by Tien Wah Press
Colour reproduction by PageSet Victoria Australia

08 09 10 11 12 6 5 4 3 2 1

Contents

Acknowledgements

Curtis Stone

Before I sit back and enjoy this book, I need to thank a few special people who have helped me to achieve it. When I was first asked to film a TV series with someone I didn't know particularly well and who had a different style of cooking to me, I naturally had some reservations. What was to unfold was a great friendship starting with a big night out with Ben and his mates when we first landed in Perth. By the end of the series and the book, I feel like he is not only my partner in crime but someone I can cook with, learn from and teach, not to mention sit up with until 7 am over a few bottles of vino talking about food for hours on end. So, Bender, thanks for everything.

Occasionally I feel privileged to be given all the amazing opportunities that I have had. Then I get a little arrogant about my life and remember the seventeen-hour days, and the six-day weeks that I put in at my first kitchen in London. I don't think I could have learnt the value of hard work from a more qualified person than Marco Pierre White, and his business partner, Jimmy La Houd.

An important side to running a restaurant like Quo Vadis is the trust you need to have in the people who work alongside you for sixteen hours a day. Without their dedication and hard work it would not be possible. Whether it is my first sous chef, Chris Hayworth, who is now the executive chef at La Rascasse in London or my second sous chef, Brendon Collins, who is now the head chef at Melisse on Venice Beach in Los Angeles or the loyal Graham Towner, who is now working with me on the new concept for a restaurant in Chelsea, London; their support has definitely helped me achieve all I have to this day.

My early inspiration came from dear Lozza, my mum; her love of good natural food will never leave me. Speaking of family I would also like to thank my father, Mr Finance, for putting a decent business head on my shoulders — this is an integral part of running any business. I come from a small family with only one brother, older than me and a bit of a tough lad. When we were younger, he gave me a few clips behind the ears, which probably gave me the strength that I have now. He is a successful businessman whom I have learnt from and for whom I have an enormous amount of respect.

One of the first chefs I worked for was Enifred Barth at the Savoy Hotel in Melbourne. He taught me the importance of tradition in food; he was very classically trained, and he passed that on to me. He is now passing on some of his knowledge, teaching at Melbourne's leading catering college, among other things, and remains a dear friend of mine.

Working on *Surfing the Menu* has been a lovely break for me from a hectic kitchen. It has given me the opportunity to broaden my knowledge and appreciation of fresh ingredients at a grass-root level — which has further inspired me in the kitchen.

I would like to thank the producer and scriptwriter — Marian and Alun Bartsch — two very driven people who brought *Surfing the Menu* to life. Furthermore, Marian put together a crew who were more professional than I thought possible, and included two brilliant stills photographers — Ewan Robinson and Craig Kinder — one of whom also had the ability to teach me to surf. Cheers Craig!

I hope you all enjoy the book as much as I have enjoyed putting it together. It would not have been possible without the creativity of a dedicated editor (Susan Morris-Yates), stylist (Kristen Anderson), photographer (Ben Dearnley), and home economists (Rebecca Truda and Jo Glynn).

Last but by no means least, I would like to thank my best mate, Chris Sheldon, who is not only the best bartender in London, but who has the ability no matter how hectic my life gets to keep a smile on my face.

Ben O'Donoghue

There are so many people I need to thank who were involved in making the TV program and the book, but more than anything else I need to say a big 'I love you' and thanks for putting up with me to my gorgeous partner, De-Arne, who single-handedly looked after our baby daughter, Ruby, for two months while I was off filming this project. You're amazing and I love you dearly.

I would also like to thank my family in Australia for always being my biggest supporters: my mum and dad; grandma; my brother Daniel and his wife Tania, and my nephew Benjie; also my new family, Peter, Jewels, Neil and Kate, for making me feel part of the family.

Thank you, Marian, for your unlimited energy and pure determination to get this all off the ground, and for having faith in Stoney and me. Also, Martine, thank you for putting up with Marian, Stoney and me (ha ha!). Thanks to the best film crew I've had the pleasure of working with (Geoff, Uli, Bubbli aka Paul, Laurie, Kelvin); to Ewan and Craig for taking the best goddamn pictures of Australia I have ever seen (mind you, you just have to point a camera in Australia and it looks great); to Kerrie for getting us all out of bed; and to Ursula for making miracles happen — you're a gem. And how can I forget Alun: you're a legend. Love those hats, mate!

To you all, four-twenty forever!

To Susan Morris-Yates, thanks a million for putting together a wonderful book over 18,000 miles away; for the many large emails too big for my hot mail account to handle, and for stretching deadlines to accommodate difficult chefs. To Ben and Kristen and Bec, thanks for all the hard work shooting the food within such a tight schedule and for putting up with the stress.

A big thank you to all the characters who appeared in the series. Herb and Gruff, thanks for the Tassie experience, and thanks to everyone else that made us so welcome. To Lozza and Golly: you're fantastic and Ruby looks beautiful in the cardie you knitted.

And finally, a big thanks to Curtis Stone for making me look good in water and bad on land!

Love to everyone I may have forgotten.

Bender

Ben O'Donoghue

BEN O'DONOGHUE

I was five when my family moved from England to Australia (for free, it now costs heaps!). My parents traveled heaps when I was young so I never saw much of England. I've always felt and sounded Australian, although I'm glad that I have a British passport, I doubt if my life would have turned out the way it has otherwise.

We moved to a town called Port Hedland in the north-west of Western Australia, one of the best places where a kid could grow up. I suppose this is where I started to cook. We'd build fires on the beach, catch fish, and cook them on corrugated iron sheets, ripped off roofs in cyclones, and bake potatoes in the coals.

When I was ten, my family moved south to Perth, where my brother and I went to school. On finishing, I got a job on Rottnest Island for the summer. I loved it so much (sun, surf, girls, etc.) that I got a job in the kitchen of the Rottnest Restaurant as a kitchen hand. This was the perfect job scenario, that is, surf-work-pub. There was great camaraderie among the chefs, and I found I had a talent in the cooking department. I thought I should get an apprenticeship. A couple of interviews later, I was working in a busy Nedlands fish restaurant called Jojo's, doing about eighty hours a week (the honeymoon was over) and loving it.

After qualifying as a chef, I was promoted to Sous Chef at Jessica's Seafood Restaurant in Perth, but felt the need to spread my wings, so I headed east to Sydney. I managed to secure a position as a Chef de Partie at a new restaurant called Goodfella's, in the inner-west suburb of Newtown. I was shortly promoted to Sous Chef. In 1993, the restaurant was awarded the Best New Restaurant Award by *The Sydney Morning Herald Good Food Guide,* and the following year two chef's hats.

Jobs and chefs come and go, and I went traveling, chasing the dream of the perfect wave. I found myself on the frost-bitten earth of old Blighty in the middle of May 1996 on my twenty-sixth birthday. I promptly bought a food guide, looked up the best restaurants in town and started looking for work. I didn't have to look for long — the second place I went to was The River Café where I somehow managed to secure a job. The River Café was the most inspirational place I've ever had the pleasure to work. The quality of chefs and the inspirational genius of Rose Gray and Ruthie Rodgers provided a highly motivated environment in which to work. Their ideas, philosophy and approach to Italian food provided the backbone of my own style of cooking.

At this time I met Jamie Oliver (yes, The Naked Chef), who had started just a few days earlier. Who was to know that Jamie's life would change so dramatically and that mine would run a similar course? During the whole Naked Chef thing, Jamie turned to his friends; to appear on *The Naked Chef* — I was on the show three times and had one episode dedicated to my birthday) — and to help out with the food styling for his first and second cookbooks as well as a publicity tour to Australia and New Zealand (on this tour I met my girlfriend and mother of my beautiful baby girl, Ruby. Thanks mate!).

After all this I made a few connections of my own, and scored an agent — thinking that a little bit of extra work and pocket money would be great from doing demos and small-bit TV appearances. The next thing, Martine, my agent is saying 'Do you want to present a show in Morocco for American TV?' I'm like, 'Yeah, love to!'

One thing led to another and I got a call to do a screen test for a new show on the BBC. I didn't think I'd get the job, especially after saying that my favourite food to cook was 'hash cookies,' but they liked my style, and my food, and the rest is history. *The Best* came along with an accompanying book for the series in April 2002 on BBC2.

To think that I was doing nothing but TV work at the time would be far from reality. I had been approached by the management of the Hyatt Carlton Tower hotel in London to be Head Chef of Monte's, a restaurant, bar and night club in the fashionable shopping area of Knightsbridge. This was a fantastic opportunity to define and refine my style and philosophy on food: approachable, relaxed, hardworking with a good sense of humour and time for play!

And now that the challenges of making *Surfing the Menu* are over, I'm looking forward to my next great adventure: taking control of the kitchen of one of the finest dining rooms in Great Britain — The Atlantic Bar and Grill.

Cooking for me is a passion and a reflex, it's something I've done since childhood and it never ceases to give pleasure or stimulate my imagination. I believe unequivocally that food should be simple and distinctive, technically and culturally correct. To say we eat with our eyes is rubbish: the senses of taste, smell and touch are far more important to me. Presentation should be secondary, but not discounted, and natural forms adhered to as much as possible. Use the best available seasonal produce, selecting from producers or suppliers with equal levels of integrity and passion as you have towards what you cook and eat.

Cooking for me is 50 per cent confidence, 40 per cent passion and 10 per cent technique and skill. Be brave and eat anything because experience is everything.

Curtis Stone

CURTIS STONE

Throughout my youth I had a few dreams. As a bit of a rebel, the Sex Pistols first inspired me to become a punk rocker. As I grew out of this, my next goal was to be up there with the best Aussie Rules footballers. Even though I had the mohawk haircut and Doc Martens, and played Aussie Rules at a good level, neither of them cut the mustard.

I have always loved eating — so much so that I consider myself greedy. I remember as a child my Mum (Lozza) baking her famous Anzac cookies*. I would watch her every move, dipping my finger into the dough at any given opportunity, waiting anxiously to get my hands on the wooden spoon while the cookies went into the oven. The smell was fantastic, I would watch them bake, anticipating their taste. Dear Lozza still sends me a batch in London from time to time.

Once it was time to get out and do some work experience I got my first real taste of how a professional kitchen worked. It was complete madness: extreme heat, long hours, sharp objects, crazy people, blood, sweat, and tears. I was excited by it and am sure I always will be. That was it, there were no more decisions to make. I did my apprenticeship at TAFE and began cooking at the Savoy Hotel in Melbourne; I spent the next five years or so working in some of Melbourne's best kitchens.

Anzac cookies are chewy rolled oats cookies. It is believed they were developed so they could be packed in food parcels and sent to the Australian and New Zealand Army Corps troops fighting in the trenches in World War 1.

But then I felt the time had come to leave Melbourne to go in search of some new challenges, so I set off to Europe with my best mate, Tomaso. Our first port of call was Calabria, Tomaso's hometown in the south of Italy. We stayed on the family farm, which was a hive of activity. Each day three generations of women would spend the entire morning preparing the family lunch: making fresh pasta, and collecting fruit and vegetables grown on the farm. The men of the family took great pride in showing me the pig, which they were fattening up to make into salamis, and the home-grown grapes, which were turned into the family wine. Their entire life revolved around their lunch, and what a lunch it was. I could talk about that summer for weeks. It consisted of good food, learning the secrets of pasta dough, home-baked breads, good wine, and the odd wild party. I think the main lesson I learnt about eating and cooking in Italy was to have respect for your raw ingredients.

My next port of call was London. In 1997 I began to work in Marco Pierre White's kitchen. Marco was Britain's most celebrated chef, the youngest chef in the world to win three Michelin stars. His reputation is deserved. He is as crazy as he is talented. Here I learnt about refined French cuisine. I started working with Spencer Patrick at the Grill Room (Café Royal), which was extremely formal. After twelve months, Marco opened a restaurant named Mirabelle, currently one of London's most famous eateries, and I was made Sous Chef there the year we won our first Michelin star. Only one year later, Marco appointed me Head Chef of another of his restaurants in London, Quo Vadis. By this time, Marco was out of the kitchen, which allowed me the freedom to incorporate more Italian influences in the food. The following year we were one of only four Italian restaurants to receive three rosette awards, and the restaurant has retained them to this day.

I loved my time at Quo Vadis, and if you ever get the chance, do eat there. I believe that good food can be as simple as using the best ingredients. I have a guy that brings me the best mozzarella from Naples every Tuesday. All I have to do is take a nice ripe tomato, chop it up, combine it with some fresh basil, salt and pepper, a drizzle of extra-virgin olive oil and put the mozzarella on top for the perfect mozzarella and tomato salad. It couldn't be simpler or more delicious.

My passion for great food has now been extended further: working with great ingredients, well produced, and at their best, has given me inspiration for a new style of restaurant. I am currently working with one of the world's leading restaurateurs, Sir Terence Conran, on an exciting new concept for London, based on ingredients, produce and respect for food.

I have eaten a lot of beautifully prepared food in my life, but one of my fondest memories is when my dad took us to Apollo Bay in southern Victoria for a summer holiday when I was about seventeen. We were sitting on a balcony overlooking the beach with a bag of shrimp, half a lemon and an ice cold Crown Lager. He said to me, 'I wonder what the poor people are doing today?' We were not a wealthy family but I did feel like the king of the world.

INTRODUCTION

Curtis: Bender and I first met when we both appeared on a BBC show
called *Saturday Kitchen*.

Ben: Yeah, and I had a bender of a hangover.

Curtis: Mate, you were no orphan, that day.

Ben: So, anyway, even though we were a little worse for wear, we had
fun together that day with the host, Gregg Wallace …

Curtis: And when Bender chose as his recipe presentation to do his
hangover cure, I knew we were going to be good mates.

Ben: Our lives working in London can sometimes be so rush, rush,
rush that sometimes I felt that I didn't have time to think.

Curtis: And in our business, that's dangerous — as new ideas, which are
the lifeblood of great menus, usually come from new experiences,
new attitudes and new people.

Ben: And every day, traveling on the same tube and the same bus can
sometimes give you tunnel vision, no pun intended.

Curtis: What I immediately found after I met Bender was that even though
so much of what we do, where we're from and what we've learnt
in our trade was so different, there was so much that we had in
common.

the beginning ...

Ben: For instance, I grew up on the west coast of Australia in Perth, starting out as a trainee school teacher. I took a part-time job in a kitchen on Rottnest Island (a holiday island just twelve kilometres off the coast) where I quickly figured out that if I could work in a restaurant and surf for the rest of the day, this would be as close to heaven as life could get ... especially if you added in girls. (Well, I was young and impressionable at that stage ...)

Curtis: Whereas, I started out doing a Bachelor of Business at university before it became clear to me that my passion was for the hot stoves of the kitchen, rather than the heat of the stock market ...

Ben: My cooking style has its roots in the Italian style.

Curtis: And mine is from a classic French perspective.

Ben: In other words, I'm a robust cook who gets into it — right up to my armpits and sometimes further ...

Curtis: And I'm a little more precise with my ingredients and my methods, shall we say.

Ben: But, the one big thing we found that we had in common when we met on that set of *Saturday Kitchen* one cold, grey, London winter's day, was that we both really needed and craved an injection of what had got us passionate about cooking in the first place. So why not go back to our roots to reconnect with the motivations of our passion ...

Curtis: … And to look for inspiration in so many of the new things that had been happening back on the other side of the world, back home in Australia.

Ben: And to fit in a surf. And girls … for Curtis, that is. I've got two beautiful girls in my life already.

Curtis: And because culinarily (is that a word?) Australia is changing at such a rapid rate … reinventing the classics and creating exciting, new genres.

Ben: And don't forget a surf.

Curtis: The clean and green environment has meant so many opportunities …

Ben: And to have a surf.

Curtis: So that's why we decided to go, together.

Ben: And to have a surf.

Curtis: So there you have it. It's all about the food and the produce.

Ben: And the surf.

Curtis: Oh yeah, and the surf … which, I must confess right up front, I'm actually not all that good at … but I'm happy to have a crack.

Ben: 'It's only practice, my son,' I said. That was all that was holding us back.

Curtis: And the fact that, at that stage, you hadn't told your partner, Dee, just yet.

Ben: A minor technicality, but as you now know, Dee being the good Aussie sort she is, gave her blessing.

    Curtis: Is that how it happened?

Ben: OK, there were some discussions and conditions, but they were minor.

    Curtis: Then you found out that Dee was pregnant with your first child!

Ben: Yeah, that was a bit of a shock. But being the good sort I previously mentioned, Dee insisted that we go, just as long as we ended up in Byron Bay, where her dad and brother and sisters live, for a party for the brand new bubby.

    Curtis: What an excellent woman. Does she have a single sister, mate?

Ben: So, that's how it all started. And in this book you can get a chance for yourself to see just how it all ended up: where we went, and some of the great people we met, the fabulous produce we found, and what inspired us to create a whole bunch of exciting new recipes.

    Curtis: Plus, I'd like you to look closely at the surfing photos that have been carefully edited to make it look as though I was moderately successful in getting up, and staying up.

Ben: You did all right, mate, you did OK.

    Curtis: Well, there's always next time …

ABOUT THE TRIP

Abrolhos Islands

BEN: Since I was a kid I'd wanted to go to the Abrolhos, a rolling three-hours boat ride off the coast of Geraldton in Western Australia. The 122 islands are clustered in three main groups off the mid-west coast. There are only a handful of places in the world that can be compared to the Abrolhos and, in many ways, even they can't be compared because this is a unique environment with some of the best coral reefs in the world. It's the home of the rock lobster industry in the west and to say that I love eating those little critters would be an understatement. The Abrolhos with their unbelievable pristine environment (think Great Barrier Reef, then add the colours of opal for the water) are also on the way out to deep water yellow and blue fin tuna fishing. These days they're also the home of a fledgling pearling industry. It's an amazing place, and the fishermen are only able to live on the islands during the lobster fishing season for a couple of months at a time in fairly basic shacks that they and their families call home. We had even thought to fit in a surf out there, too, but on the day Captain Murray took us out to the break, three gigantic tiger sharks slid under the boat when we'd stopped. So, Curtis and I decided that going back to camp and ending the day with a beer was a better idea than ending up with the words 'shark bait' on our tombstones.

Broome

CURTIS: Even in Melbourne we'd heard about Broome up north in the Kimberley region of Western Australia. Up here it's not summer and winter, it's wet season and dry season with, as we found, some Broome-only seasons too. Plenty of rain, loads of sunshine, and rich red soils guarantee that you can grow pretty much anything you want up here; where life seems as close to ideal as it can get. Catch fabulous fish off the beach or delicious mud cabs in the mangroves near town for dinner. Another great thing is the truly remarkable mixture of cultures that make up Broome, most of its inhabitants having originally being attracted here by the pearling industry that survives, and thrives today. So, mix all of them together: the unbelievable environment, the delicious produce, plus a group of people descendent from Malays, Japanese, South Sea Islanders, Europeans and Australian Aborigines and you've got a recipe for a remarkable and memorable visit.

Hunter Valley

CURTIS: I love great wine, and when you combine it with great food, I'm in heaven. So an opportunity to put the two together again on this trip (Margaret River, New Norcia, Tasmania and the Hunter Valley) was too good an opportunity to pass up. The Hunter Valley is about a two-hour drive north of Sydney, and extends way up into the Barrington Tops. The region is lush and green, and the rich volcanic soils, and the regular rainfall have ensured that parts of it look more like Wales than the classic image of Australia. There are great vineyards there, and so, purely in the interests of research, we took the opportunity to sample as many of them as we could. We met some great and passionate characters and we even did some horse riding while helping the stockmen round up the herd on a cattle station in the Barrington Tops. Thankfully, I am to horse riding what Bender is to surfing, so this was my turn to shine. Hi-ho Silver, away!

New Norcia

CURTIS: I had read about a Spanish monastery town, just 82 miles (132 kilometres north) of Perth in Western Australia, called New Norcia. Founded by Dom Salvado in 1846, New Norcia is today home for sixteen Benedictine monks. The architecture, with its strong Spanish flavour, dominates the Australian bush setting, and the buildings are classsified by the National Trust. I was interested to see it for myself because of the Mediterranean influence (even to this day they produce the three Mediterranean staples of bread, wine and olives, and they still observe an afternoon siesta). Very civilized, I think. Ben told me he had played Aussie Rules footy there when he was a schoolkid, so that settled it, we had to check it out. Plus we were a hundred ks from the ocean, so there was no chance for Ben to show me up again in the surf. New Norcia is in the middle of what the West Australians call the 'wheat belt' — mile after mile of rolling pastures and wheat plains with sheep and cattle everywhere, and quite a few surprises, too.

Margaret River

BEN: When I was growing up in Perth, we'd often come to Margaret River to surf, party, and play up. It's only a three-and-a-half-hour drive south from Perth to some of Western Australia's best beaches. Since I've been away, the whole region has become a gourmet's delight with world-class produce: including game, seafood, vegetables, and fruit, not to mention wine. A buddy of mine, Aaron Carr, whom I did my apprenticeship with, is now Head Chef at Vasse Felix — so that means surf-time and, for old time's sake, party-time too. The region is bound on three sides by ocean, so the climate is mild. In between the towering forests, beautiful lush, green farmlands grow fabulous produce. With over sixty wineries in the region, it's not hard to get a drink either.

Tasmania

BEN: Ah, beautiful Tassie. What can I tell you about it that you don't already know? It's an island off the south-eastern tip of Australia. It looks more like Europe than Australia with its lush farmland, pure freshwater streams, and spectacular mountains. They make some great beer there, the wines are pretty good, and everything else is special, too. This was not my first trip there, I'd visited, and stayed with Gruff and Sandra a number of times before, as they were the parents of a mate I shared a house with for a few years in Sydney. So I was pretty familiar with the place, and I thought it appropriate that I show Curtis around. I have surfed there in the past, but because it was a fair old drive from where we were staying in beautiful Strahan, we didn't get the boards off the roof. Hope we didn't look like poseurs driving around …

Bellarine Peninsula

CURTIS: The Bellarine Peninsula, just 15 miles (24 kilometres) south of Geelong, outside of Melbourne, is where I did a fair amount of growing up, and that seemed like a good reason to visit, and show Bender some special places. The clincher for Ben was that there are sensational beaches all along the coast. It's even called the Surf Coast from just outside the historic town of Queenscliffe all the way along the Great Ocean Road. Bells Beach at Torquay is where one of the major surf comps in Australia is held every year. There are loads of produce surprises, too. The biggest surprise of the trip was that I was under the impression that Bender and I were going to cater for a party my mother was hosting, but there was something cooking between Lozza and Bender that I wasn't aware of — and that was a surprise party for me! It was great fun, although much of the party itself is something of a blur. I'm sure someone will have some incriminating photographs to help me out, which are bound to be brought out at an inappropriate time. Oh well …

Byron Bay

BEN: I had been to Byron Bay with Dee, my partner, on many occasions before. This time was different, however. I was to meet Dee there and reconnect with our brand-new beautiful daughter, Ruby, who had flown from England to meet Dee's family for the first time. So, as you can imagine, as Curtis and I flew into Coolangatta (about an hour's drive away from Byron Bay), I was a little nervous. When I saw my two favourite girls in the airport, my heart melted. See, I'm just a big softie! Byron Bay is absolutely beautiful — it's where the rainforest meets the sea. The rich volcanic soils of the surrounding countryside mean sensational produce, and spectacular scenery. Curtis and I found some great seafood, macadamia nuts and oils, excellent pork, and some pretty special coffee, too. All this came together at a family gathering Curtis helped me cater for: a bloody fantastic barbecue on a deck overlooking a rainforest creek. How good is that? Hard to beat, I say.

Abrolhos Islands

Abrolhos Islands

Lobsters, Tuna, and Boschettis

Ben O'Donoghue

If you point a boat due west from the coast of Geraldton in Western Australia, two or three hours later you'll run smack bang into the Abrolhos Islands. I reckon the description 'island' flatters them, as they're in fact flat coral plateaus, less than a metre or two above sea level, mostly devoid of vegetation. That's what's left of most of the islands after the British took Chinese workers there to remove rich guano more than a century ago.

The Abrolhos are rich in maritime history, too. More than sixty sailing ships have smashed into the coral reefs. The most famous shipwreck, but by no means the first, was the Dutch vessel *Batavia* in 1629. Driven forward at a great rate of knots by the Roaring Forties from the Cape of Good Hope in South Africa, the *Batavia* (like all the others shipwrecked) left its turn north to head for the Spice Islands of Indonesia too late. What followed after the ship broke apart on the reefs was mutiny and massacre: 125 men, women and children were slaughtered in drunken, sun-crazed binges. Captain Pelsaert escaped in a boat and rowed 1000 miles (1600 kilometres) north to Batavia (now Jakarta). Remarkably, he made it. He then returned with a platoon of soldiers to sort out the mutineers. Having survived six months on these islands, it probably means the mutineers were the first unofficial European settlers in Australia.

The name Abrolhos apparently comes from the Portuguese 'Abrios Oi-os', which means, 'keep your eyes open'. So much for the short history lesson!

Our 35-mile (55-kilometre) trip to the Abrolhos from Geraldton, which took a little over three hours, was uneventful, if a little rough. Our 50-foot (16-metre) converted tuna fishing vessel, with Captain Murray stoically at the helm, ploughed through the oncoming swell, spraying Curtis and me until we were soaked. But we couldn't feel too sorry for ourselves because we knew that in the early days, fishermen would come to the island in all weather in open sail-rigged dinghies!

North Island

Wallabi Group

East Wallabi Island

Webbe Hayes Fort **x**

Beacon Island

x *Wreck of the Batavia*

West Wallabi Island

INDIAN OCEAN

Easter Group

Leo's Island

Rat Island

Suomi Island

Wooded Island

Basile Island

Gun Island

Middle Island

Pelsaert Island

Pelsaert Group

Off in the distance we caught our first glimpse of the islands, low and flat on the horizon. They looked surreal, a little like a mirage. The waters surrounding the Abrolhos are as clear as crystal, and the reefs and fish schools are seen through the jade and sapphire waters. Pods of dolphin frolic, seals and sea lions sunbake and giant manta rays loll about in the shallows. The ocean here is a constant 72°F (22°C) all year round, which means that the lobsters love it, tropical fish abound, and the reefs of coral thrive to rival the Great Barrier Reef in beauty. That means sharks, too, but more about that later.

We headed off to the Abrolhos because this is one of the main lobster fisheries on the west coast. One hundred and fifty licensed fishermen are allowed to take up residence on just twenty-two of the 122 islands that stretch nearly 60 miles (100 kilometres) in length. Crude shacks (or camps as they're called) are their homes for the five months of the season, and work is why they're here. Without an invitation, it's simply not possible to stay on the islands. During the annual season around 10,000 tonnes of western rock lobster are caught, many ending up on fine dining tables around the world.

We moored at one of the many jetties on Basile Island, one of the islands in the Southern Group, which boasts about twenty camps. Basile was first settled by Italian fishermen, and the names of the second- and third-generation rock lobster fishermen and women are evidence of that. Some of the other islands have built a pub or a community hall for the residents; on Basile Island they built a little church. The Archbishop of Geraldton visits and holds mass there twice a year.

On the island we were met by Pia Boschetti. Pia's father first came to the Abrolhos in the 1950s. Today Pia runs the family's pearl farm; sister Erica runs the family's tuna and swordfish fishing arm; and brother Michael fishes for lobster, and trawls for school fish from his huge modern boat.

With so many of the Boschetti family there, I thought it would be nice to hold a family dinner, and invite a few of the other people we met. That meant we'd need some food and, as fresh is best, we headed off in a jetboat to a secret spot on one of the islands that Murray Davidson knows. The jetboat is flat-bottomed so we were able to take short cuts across reefs where there was maybe only a foot or so of water. This means that the lobster pots can be placed in otherwise inaccessible waters, especially close in where the swell is breaking over the reef. It's the most dangerous place for a boat to be, and where lots of rock lobsters like to live. Just at the point the waves break is where the pots are lowered by rope. Their spots are marked by blue floats. Hauling the pots up into the boat can be quite heavy work if you have a few hefty lobsters inside!

On the way out to the secret spot, Murray asked if we'd like to go for a surf. Curtis and I were stoked, and the waves Murray showed us were fantastic. We couldn't wait to get into the water, but as we were getting into our wetties, I glanced over the side just as three tiger sharks slid by. This is not a fisherman's story — they were huge, bloody huge and, as neither of us is crazy, we decided discretion was the better part of valour. After all, the place is not called Bitey Holes for nothing!

We also had a chance to drop a fishing line with a lure. The fish around the Abrolhos are amazing. We think Curtis hooked a big fighting Spanish mackerel — his fishing rod bent and the reel screamed like crazy before there was a crack! and the line snapped, letting the fish swim away in triumph. Spanish mackerel grow to over 3 feet (1 metre) in length here. I left my line in and soon had a strike, too — a lovely coral trout. Anywhere else in the world it would have been a pretty big fish but here it was a tiddler in comparison to the other fish we'd seen, so we threw it back.

Murray said he'd show us a good-sized fish, so we made a detour into his camp. In the water beside the wharf he swished around a few leftover lobster shells. It wasn't long before a large bald-chin grouper appeared. This, Murray told us, was Pete, his pet, who'd been coming around for several months, striking up a friendship. Pete was no ordinary fish. Before he'd feed, he'd lift his head out of the water and take a good look at Murray and me. Then, after he'd eaten the leftovers, he would swim in a circle and float on his back to let Murray and me scratch his stomach, just like a cat or dog.

We eventually arrived at the secret island after our surfing and fishing detours. Every part of the surface of every coral face above and below the water we could see was covered with oysters! Unbelievable. The locals take a screwdriver with them, jemmy off the top shell, scoop the oyster into it with an oyster knife, squeeze over a little lemon and slurp it down. These are the freshest oysters I have ever tasted, and they were bloody brilliant. As always with seafood, the simpler you treat the produce, the better. That was certainly the case here. If I'd had a cold bottle of Riesling, I reckon I could have spent the day there. Heaven!

The downside was that, as we couldn't prise the whole shell off, there was no way to safely and hygienically transport these plump little beauties back to camp. So we had a few more for luck, then sat down to have a think.

Pia got on the phone to Erica, who has boats fishing further out to sea near the continental shelf. Erica had a boat on the way into port at that moment so we ordered a fresh tuna from her and headed back to camp. The thought of a full fresh tuna was enough to send me into a spin of recipe ideas and taste combinations. By the time we'd reached the jetty I knew exactly what I was going to do. So did Curtis, but he needed one further ingredient that we didn't have — fresh tomatoes.

When the Chinese workers were here they brought with them numerous vegetables and plants. These days, after the rains, descendent tomatoes self-seed and self-sow in the crevices of a few small islands. Murray knew just where to look. Again we climbed on board the jetboat and took off at a great rate of knots. Not long afterwards we pulled up at an island. Murray jumped onto the beach and we duly followed. Not long into our walk, there they were: small, plump, red, and pure — just as they would have grown more than a century before when they were first brought to these islands.

Back on dry land I was introduced to Perry Minissale. (Everyone on Basile Island has an Italian name and heritage.) Perry's a great guy and he showed us how he puts his catch into a holding pen to await the arrival of the supply boat, which takes the catch back to the mainland. Perry's pride and joy is Melissa, a painted mermaid that has been passed around between the fishermen who live on the islands. Perry lives alone out there. Except for Melissa that is.

At dinner, we not only had a sensational meal but it was accompanied by one of the most spectacular sunsets I have ever seen. According to the locals, 'That was nothing, you should have seen the sunset last week!' The dinner was a resounding success and even though our guests have been eating their produce for generations, we were still able to surprise them with new tastes, combinations, and textures. I was stoked, especially by the comments made by Bert, Pia, and Erica's dad.

What really impressed me about these islands was the fact that there are quotas and enforceable rules in place to ensure that this environment stays absolutely pristine and pure. The rock lobsters that leave here carry the Marine Stewardship Council tag, which means that they are from a certified sustainable environment — a great endorsement. The best specimens are kept alive, and flown first class around the world to end up being served fresh at the best tables.

While Pia, Erica, and Michael are second-generation Abrolhos Island workers, this attitude to long-term sustainability ensures that there will be the same opportunities for their children, and their children's children. I reckon that's bloody great!

Rock oysters with Champagne jelly

What can I say about oysters and Champagne? I like to eat such exquisite seafood very simply, and this is a match made in heaven. Champagne and wines can be turned into jellies so simply. For instance, Madeira works beautifully with chicken liver parfait. All this means is that you can now enjoy in food what you usually enjoy out of a glass.

SERVES 4

24	rock oysters (any oysters will do), freshly opened	24
1¼ cups	Champagne	300 mL
½ tbsp	gelatin	7.5mL
3 lb	rock salt	1.5 kg
7 fl oz	water	200 mL
1 cup	loosely packed watercress leaves	250 mL

1 Remove the oysters from their shells, and place in a bowl with their juices. Cover with plastic wrap, and transfer to the refrigerator. Clean and dry the shells.

2 Pour the Champagne into a saucepan. Sprinkle the gelatin over the Champagne and allow to soften for a few minutes. Place over a low heat and stir until the gelatin dissolves. Remove from the heat.

3 Slightly moisten the rock salt with the water, and spread on a tray large enough to hold the oysters in a single layer. Place the oyster shells on top so that they are sitting level. Pour enough Champagne into each shell to half fill. Chill in the refrigerator until set.

4 Chill any remaining jelly in a small container in the refrigerator, too. Once set, break up this jelly using a fork.

5 Place 3–4 leaves of watercress at the back of each shell. Place an oyster on the jelly, and then spoon a small amount of the broken-up jelly at the back of the oyster shell.

Curtis Stone

Abrolhos Island rock oysters

We had the opportunity to grab some local rock oysters, and the residents had pointed out a clump of self-seeding bush tomatoes, so it occurred to me to put a twist on a dish I do as Head Chef at Monte's in London.

SERVES 4

48	rock oysters (any oysters will do), freshly opened	48

Dressing

1 lb	cherry tomatoes, cut in half	500 g
2 tsp	chopped fresh thyme	10 mL
1 tsp	finely chopped fresh flat-leaf parsley	5 mL
1/2 tsp	finely chopped fresh tarragon	2 mL
1	clove garlic, minced	1
	Salt and freshly ground black pepper to taste	
1 tbsp	HP sauce	15 mL
1 tbsp	sherry vinegar	15 mL
2 tsp	freshly squeezed lime juice	10 mL
	hot pepper sauce to taste	
1/3 cup	light olive oil	75 mL
1 tbsp	freshly grated horseradish to garnish	15 mL

1. Ensure that the oysters are detached from their shell. Cover, and keep chilled until ready to serve.

2. To make the dressing, place the tomatoes, thyme, parsley, tarragon, and garlic in a bowl, and season with salt and pepper. Set aside to marinate for 30 minutes. Transfer to a food processor, and purée, then strain through a sieve to extract the juice. Mix this juice with the HP sauce, vinegar, lime juice and hot pepper sauce, then whisk in the olive oil. Chill before serving.

3. Arrange the oysters on crushed ice to keep them cold, and spoon over enough dressing to cover each oyster. Garnish with a little horseradish, and serve at once.

Tuna ceviche with aromatic salad

Buy a nice very fresh piece of tuna from your fishmonger. Things to look for are a deep red colour, firm smooth flesh that doesn't appear dull or watery, and the cut surface should have a rainbow-like shimmer across it. Always have a smell; it should be fresh, and a little salty.

SERVES 4–6

Marinade

²/₃ cup	freshly squeezed lime juice	150 mL
1 tsp	sesame oil	5 mL
1 tbsp	palm sugar (jaggery)*	15 mL
1 tbsp	soy sauce	15 mL
1 tbsp	coconut milk	15 mL

Garnish

7 fl oz	vegetable oil	200 mL
3¹/₂ oz	Asian shallots, finely sliced lengthways	100 g
3	cloves garlic, finely sliced lengthways	3
¹/₂ tsp	sea salt	2 mL
¹/₂ tsp	sugar	2 mL

Salad

3 cups	loosely packed frisée; purple basil; small curly endive; mint and baby basil leaves	750 mL
¹/₂ cup	fresh coriander leaves	125 mL
1 lb	fresh tuna	500 g
2	avocados, diced	2
	Salt and freshly ground black pepper to taste	
1 tsp	freshly squeezed lemon juice	5 mL

* Available at specialist Asian food shops.

1. To make the marinade, mix all the ingredients together in a ceramic bowl.

2. To prepare the garnish, heat ²/₃ cup (150 mL) oil in a small saucepan. Fry the shallots and garlic separately until golden. Be aware that the colour will increase after they have been fried. Remove with a slotted spoon, place on paper towels, and set aside to drain, and cool. Grind the fried shallots and garlic with the salt and sugar in a mortar and pestle to give a crumbly texture.

3. To make the salad, rinse and drain the frisée, basil, endive, mint, and coriander leaves. Transfer to a bowl, cover with plastic wrap, and place in the refrigerator until required.

4. Using a very sharp knife, neatly cut the tuna into ¹/₃-inch (8-mm) slices. Place in the marinade, covering all the slices well, and leave for 5 minutes. Season the avocados with salt and pepper, and toss with the lemon juice. Gently drain the tuna, then arrange on a serving plate. Top with the avocado, and drizzle over a little of the remaining oil. Toss the last of the oil with the salad leaves, and arrange on top of the avocado.

5. Sprinkle the garnish over the salad, and serve at once.

Rock lobster tagliatelle with fennel and truffle oil

The Abrolhos Islands produce some of the best rock lobsters in the world, and, from my experience cooking overseas, I've yet to taste a lobster to match these. I like to use fresh truffles at work but here truffle oil works well; just don't use too much! This recipe is a special occasion dish.

SERVES 4

4	live rock lobsters (any lobster will do), weighing 1 lb (500 g) each	4
2	baby fennel bulbs	2
1/3 cup	unsalted butter	75 mL
4 dashes	truffle oil	4
1/4 cup	freshly squeezed lemon juice or to taste	50 mL
1 lb	fresh tagliatelle	500 g
	Salt and freshly ground black pepper to taste	

1 Place the lobsters in the freezer for 20 minutes.

2 Discard the tough outer leaves of the fennel bulbs, reserving the green feathery tops for garnish. Slice the bulbs into thin wedges 1/2-inch (1-cm) thick on the outside edge. Reserve.

3 Put a large saucepan of salted water on to boil, add the lobsters, and when the water returns to the boil cook for 8–10 minutes. Remove the lobsters with tongs, and keep the water on the boil. When the lobsters are cool enough to handle, separate the head from the body, and remove the meat from the tail. Dice, and reserve the meat. Using a spoon, scoop out all the flesh and coral from the head. Force this through a sieve into a small saucepan. Mix in 3–4 tbsp (45–60 mL) boiling water, and add the butter. Place on low heat to melt the butter, and heat through. If the sauce is too thin, continue cooking until it reduces. Remove from the heat, and whisk in the truffle oil and lemon juice.

4 Meanwhile, put the fennel wedges and tagliatelle into the boiling water, and cook until al dente. Drain, and return to the pan. Season with salt and pepper. Add the reserved diced lobster meat, pour in the sauce, and toss to coat. Serve with a sprinkling of chopped fennel tops.

Char-grilled sardines with cranberry bean salad

This is a dish that needs to be eaten in the sun. I first ate sardines grilled like this in the south of France, sitting outside near the water. They eat particularly well with cranberry beans. This is really healthy food, and is just right for the Australian climate.

SERVES 4

Marinade

	Finely grated rind of 2 lemons	
1 tbsp	chopped fresh thyme leaves	15 mL
10	cloves garlic, minced	10
1/4 cup	olive oil	50 mL
8	large sardines	8
14 oz	fresh cranberry beans in the pod, shelled	400 g
2 cups	chicken stock	500 mL
2	vine-ripened tomatoes	2
1 cup	chopped fresh flat-leaf parsley	250 mL
5	cloves garlic, minced	5
	Finely grated rind of 2 lemons	
	Finely grated rind of 2 limes	
	Finely grated rind of 1 orange	
1/3 cup	extra-virgin olive oil	75 mL
	Sea salt and freshly ground black pepper	

1. Mix all the marinade ingredients together.

2. Fillet the sardines, leaving them joined at the tail. Place on a dish, and coat with the marinade. Cover with plastic wrap, and refrigerate for 12 hours.

3. Place the beans and chicken stock in a saucepan. Bring to the boil, and simmer for 25–30 minutes, until beans are soft. Remove from the heat, and allow to cool in the stock.

4. Core the tomatoes, and cut a cross on their tops. Plunge into a pot of boiling water for 10–12 seconds. Remove, and cool in ice water for 1 minute before peeling. Squeeze out the seeds, and dice the flesh. Place in a large bowl. Drain, and rinse the beans, and combine with the tomatoes.

5. Combine the parsley, garlic and lemon, lime and orange rind in a bowl. Stir in the extra-virgin olive oil, and season with salt and pepper. Toss half through the bean and tomato salad. Pile the salad in the centre of 4 serving plates.

6. Preheat a char-grill to very hot. Grill the sardines for 2 minutes skin-side down, then turn and cook for a further 30 seconds. Arrange 2 sardines per serving in a cross on top of the salad. Serve, drizzled with the remaining parsley dressing.

Curtis Stone

Barbecued rock lobster with garlic butter and Béarnaise sauce

I simply love cooking with a fantastic creature like lobster. The Canadian and European lobsters are brilliant to use, and would work perfectly with this recipe. The important thing to remember when cooking lobster is that the water must not be too hot; around 160°F (70°C) is perfect. This temperature will allow the lobster meat to relax as it cooks.

Whenever I cook with lobster, I feel privileged to be using such first-class ingredients, so I always treat these ingredients with the respect they deserve.

SERVES 4

2	green rock lobsters (any lobster will do), weighing about 2 lb (1 kg) each	2
2	small carrots, roughly chopped	2
2	celery stalks, chopped	2
1	leek, thickly sliced	1
1	lemon, roughly chopped	
1	head garlic, unpeeled, roughly chopped	1
1	onion, roughly chopped	1
4 cups	water	1 L
7 fl oz	garlic butter (see recipe opposite)	200 mL
1/3 cup	Béarnaise sauce (see recipe opposite)	75 mL
	Fresh chervil sprigs to serve	

1. Place the lobsters in the freezer for 20 minutes.

2. Combine the carrots, celery, leek, lemon, garlic, onion and water in a large saucepan, place over medium heat, and bring to 160°F (70°C), a very slow simmer. Add the lobsters, and poach for 5–8 minutes, depending on their size. Remove from the water, and rest for 5 minutes.

3. Preheat the barbecue. Using a large knife, split the lobsters in half lengthways. Remove the meat from the tail, and slice into smaller pieces. Pipe about 2 tbsp (30 mL) garlic butter into the shells. Replace the lobster meat, then pipe the remaining garlic butter over the top.

4. Transfer the tails in their shells to the hot barbecue. Close the lid, and cook for 4–5 minutes. If the barbecue has no lid, cover the tails loosely with foil. Remove from the heat, and spoon Béarnaise sauce over the top. Garnish with chervil for serving.

continued opposite...

Curtis Stone

Garlic butter

1 cup	unsalted butter, softened	250 mL
1 tbsp	finely chopped shallots	15 mL
4	cloves garlic, minced	4
2 tsp	chopped fresh flat-leaf parsley	10 mL
1 tsp	pastis, such as Pernod	5 mL
	Salt and freshly ground black pepper	

1 Mix the butter in a bowl with the shallots, garlic, parsley and pastis, and season with salt and pepper. Spoon into a piping bag fitted with a wide nozzle.

Béarnaise sauce

2	shallots, chopped	2
5	white peppercorns	5
1 cup	dry white wine	250 mL
2 cups	white wine vinegar	500 mL
4	sprigs tarragon	4
4	free-range egg yolks	4
2/3 cup	clarified butter	150 mL
	Salt and freshly ground white pepper	
20	tarragon leaves, finely chopped	20

1 To make the reduction, place the shallots, peppercorns, wine, vinegar, and 2 sprigs of tarragon in a saucepan, and bring to the boil. Simmer for 20 minutes, or until reduced by three-quarters. Add the remaining sprigs of tarragon, then remove from heat. Cool, then chill in the refrigerator until cold. (This can be kept for 1 week.)

2 Strain the reduction. Place 2 tbsp (30 mL) in a stainless steel bowl, and add the egg yolks. Place the bowl over a pan of simmering water, and whisk vigorously. Continue whisking until the mixture thickens to form a light, foamy sabayon. Remove from the heat.

3 Melt the butter, slowly pour it into the sabayon in a steady stream, whisking continually. Season to taste with salt and pepper. Line a coarse sieve with a piece of muslin, and push the sauce through into a bowl.

4 Mix the tarragon leaves into the sauce.

Curtis Stone

Coral trout poached in milk, lemon, basil, and white wine

This is great served with creamy mashed potato or pea purée, or, as I do at the restaurant, with potato and ricotta dumplings (see following page), which are a bit like gnocchi.

SERVES 4

1 tbsp	vegetable oil	15 mL
4	fresh coral trout (or use sea bass or scorpion fish) fillets, weighing about 6 oz (175 g) each	4
	Salt and freshly ground black pepper	
	Finely grated rind of 1 lemon	
1	dried chili	1
1	clove garlic, finely sliced	1
1/2 cup	dry white wine	125 mL
2 cups	skim milk	500 mL
2 tbsp	mascarpone cheese	30 mL
4 tbsp	chopped fresh basil	60 mL

1 In a saucepan large enough to accommodate the fish fillets in a single layer, warm the oil over low heat. Season the fillets with salt and pepper, and place in the pan. Seal on both sides, without colouring the flesh. Add the lemon rind, chili and garlic, and fry gently for 1–2 minutes, to allow the flavours to develop.

2 Add the wine and milk, increase the heat, and bring to the boil. Reduce to a very gentle simmer, and cover, with the lid gaping slightly. Poach the fillets for 4–8 minutes, depending on their thickness, until just cooked through. When done, the flesh will flake when pressed gently. The sauce will appear slightly curdled. Remove from the heat, and transfer the fish to warm serving plates. Add the mascarpone to the pan, and stir into the sauce. Taste for seasoning and add the basil at the last minute. Serve the trout with plenty of sauce spooned over the top.

Ben O'Donoghue

Potato and ricotta dumplings

I like to call these dumplings rather than gnocchi because they contain a filling.

SERVES 4–6

1 lb	floury potatoes, scrubbed	500 g
1	large free-range egg	1
	Salt and freshly ground black pepper	
Pinch	freshly ground nutmeg	
3½ oz	all-purpose flour (approx)	100 g
2¾ oz	ricotta cheese	75 g
1 tbsp	finely chopped fresh basil	15 mL

1 Boil the potatoes in their skins for about 30 minutes, until cooked through. Drain, and peel while hot. Press through a sieve into a large bowl. While still hot, add the egg, beating lightly until combined. Season with salt, pepper, and nutmeg. Gradually incorporate the flour, stopping once a firm but light dough forms. Knead for 30 or so seconds, until just smooth.

2 Mix the ricotta with the basil. Roll the dough out onto a floured surface to a thickness of ⅛ inch (3 mm). Using a cookie cutter or an upturned glass, cut out 2-inch (5-cm) discs. Place a small teaspoonful of the ricotta mixture in the centre of a disc and cover with another disc of dough. Press the edges to seal.

3 Bring a large saucepan of salted water to the boil. Cook the dumplings, a few at a time, for about 1 minute, until they float to the surface. Remove with a slotted spoon, and serve with the Coral Trout Poached in Milk, Lemon, Basil and White Wine (see previous page).

Ben O'Donoghue

Barbecued hot and sour tuna escalopes

This quick and easy way of marinating fish is perfect for a summer barbecue, however, it is also lovely to pan-fry indoors. This marinade is also great for shrimp, and most firm fish.

SERVES 4

Marinade

2 tbsp	chopped shallots	30 mL
2 tbsp	minced garlic	30 mL
2 tbsp	peeled and minced fresh ginger	30 mL
2 tbsp	chopped chili (depending upon heat)	30 mL
2 tbsp	crushed fresh lemongrass	30 mL
	Grated rind of 1 lime	
2 tbsp	freshly squeezed lime juice	30 mL
2 tbsp	chopped fresh mint	30 mL
2 tbsp	chopped fresh basil	30 mL
2 tbsp	chopped fresh coriander	30 mL
4	tuna escalopes, weighing about 5 oz (150 g) each	4
1 tbsp	olive oil	15 mL
	Mixed salad leaves, to serve	

❶ Place all the marinade ingredients in a large bowl, and mix well.

❷ Add the tuna, and rub the marinade over the escalopes. Cover with plastic wrap, and chill for 30 minutes.

❸ Preheat the barbecue or grill. Add the olive oil to the tuna, and gently toss to coat. Remove the tuna, and barbecue for about 45 seconds on each side, until cooked through. Serve on a bed of salad leaves.

Curtis Stone

Tropical fruits poached in mango wine

Tropical fruits are perfect to eat in summer. I love poaching fruits. If you can't find mango wine you could use fruit juice or stock syrup of 4 cups (1 L) water, 1 lb (500 g) sugar, and the juice of 3 lemons with some puréed mango to your taste.

SERVES 4–6

6 cups	mango wine	1.5 L
1	cinnamon stick	1
4	kiwi fruit, peeled	4
6	lichees, peeled	6
	Cheeks of 2 mangoes, peeled	2
1	small papaya, peeled, quartered and seeded	1
1	honeydew melon, peeled, quartered and seeded	1
4-inch	piece of fresh ginger, peeled	10-cm
1 cup	tightly packed fresh mint leaves	250 mL

1. Place all but $1/3$ cup (75 mL) of the mango wine in a large saucepan. Add the cinnamon, and bring to the boil. Add the kiwi fruit, lichees, mango cheeks, papaya, and honeydew melon. Lower the heat, and simmer gently for 3–5 minutes. Remove the fruit with a slotted spoon, and spread on a large platter to cool. Using a mortar and pestle, pound the ginger and mint with the remaining wine. Leave to infuse.

2. Spoon out half of the poaching liquid, and save for another use. Bring the remaining half to the boil, and reduce to $1/2$ cup (125 mL).

3. Slice the fruit and arrange on a serving platter. Drizzle the reduction over the top.

4. Strain the infused wine, and pour over the fruit before serving.

Note: The excess poaching liquid can be made into a jelly. Soak 1 gelatin leaf per 3 1/2 fl oz (100 ml) of liquid in cold water until soft. Squeeze dry and stir into the warmed poaching liquid. Pour into moulds and set in the refrigerator.

Curtis Stone

Broome

Broome

Muddies, Pearls, and Mangoes

Curtis Stone

Thanks largely to the pearling industry, which began in the early 1870s, Broome is a melting pot of many cultures: Chinese, Japanese, Malay, Pacific Islander, and Aboriginal. As a result, Broome has become a harmonious fusion between the cultures and cuisines of the West and the East. This is what we expected before we arrived. What surprised us, though, was the natural fusion that has occurred between the European and Asian ways of life, and that of the traditional values of the Australian Aboriginal people.

As we entered Broome, we took a drive through Chinatown. A collection of buildings and stores showed that the oriental influence is still very evident. My first impressions of Broome were of the heat and the colours. It is hot, tropical, a little humid, and this dictates the pace at which things get done. Here they call that 'Broome time.'

Colours, vibrant primary colours. The coastline is spectacular. The ocean is an iridescent, opal green. The sky is a rich, endless blue. The greens are tropical, bold, and lush. And the soil is red, really red. Deep, dark ochre, and red. It's spellbinding, too. No wonder people are drawn back here time and time again, and others find it hard to leave.

Our Broome adventure really began after we met Baamba. Baamba's a local Aboriginal character. He's an actor, a singer, and a know-all about who's who and where to get everything. He's been married four times, and has a heap of grandkids. He loves good food, so on that count alone we were destined to be good friends.

Baamba is in touch with his heritage and culture, and was able to tell us so much about the traditional way of life, the basis of which is being in touch with nature and the environment. Simple things, such as knowing mud crabs don't come out from their mangrove lairs in a full moon, as their camouflage is rendered less than ideal, can mean the difference between a good

INDIAN OCEAN

Willie Creek
Pearl Farm

BROOME

Roebuck Bay

Great Northern Highway

feed, and an empty stomach. As can essential things like where crocs hide, where turtles lay eggs, and where water can be found in the desert.

Another thing we learned was that a bro (brother or close friend) is called a bubbli. After we'd proven ourselves, we too became referred to as bubblis. 'Hey bubbli!' was the favoured greeting.

We noticed the 'Broome time' phenomenon means that when you want to do something, that's the right time. When you want to leave, that's the right time to leave. When you want to eat, that's the right time to eat. I think in Spanish-speaking countries they have something similar called mañana.

Broome time is not only about clock time, they have their own seasons too: wet season, and dry season. When it rains in the wet season, it's almost a solid wall of water. There's no point running for shelter, you'll be drenched within seconds, and you might as well pull off the road if you're in the car, as you'll be virtually driving blind. As suddenly as it begins, it's over. The seasons then break down further, into barramundi season (barra being one of the very best fish to eat), and mango season, for instance. Everyone in town also knows when it's high tide, or low. In Broome, that's important to know because the tides dictate most activities, as there can be up to a 27-foot (9-metre) rise and fall. It's not an unusual occurrence for the unwary to park their car on the beach, and come back hours later to find it washed away! Plus, the tides dictate when you go fishing: the best fishing is on the neap tide, when the variation between the high and low tide is at its minimum. This is real integration with the ebb and flow of nature. Not fighting it, but going with the current. That's part of the Aboriginal culture that the entire town and, probably, region have adopted. As a general observation, it may also be the reason why the Aboriginal people have been able to survive and prosper for thousands of years in such a harsh and unforgiving land.

We asked Baamba if we could get some mud crabs, and he knew exactly where to take us. Catching mud crabs might sound like fun, but a clue to what it was really like is contained in the name. We waited until low tide, and then headed out into the mud where the mangroves grow. Mud. Icky, sticky, and knee deep. But if you catch your muddies, it's all worthwhile.

With the help of a long piece of wire — which is used to prod the mud until you detect it clicking on a shell, and then to coax the muddy from its hole, being careful to avoid its nipping claws — we got the crabs into a bucket, and back to dry land, ready for culinary inspiration.

Barramundi is a local native fish, popular throughout Australia. It has a superb firm flesh that poaches, grills, or bakes beautifully. Baamba took us down to the town boat ramp where a bubbli of Baamba's had just docked his fishing vessel. Baamba 'hoied' his mate Milton, and we clambered aboard. Luckily, they were just sorting the catch, and among it were some fantastic fresh barramundi and threadfin salmon that we took with us.

On the town beach we caught sight of Pete's Noodle Bus. Malay-born Pete's quite famous around here, and, after a snack, we decided to get some of his fresh noodles.

Broome's Cable Beach is famous for two things. The first is the Cable Station, built here in 1889, that was the terminus of the undersea cable link between Australia and Java. The second is camels, which visitors can ride along the beach at dawn and dusk. Some important points to know about camels are that they have very poor dental hygiene, so their breath could remove paint, and they can't see behind them, as Bender found out when one camel stepped on his foot. You should have seen him jump.

Another bubbli of Baamba's was Arno, who grows mangoes. Baamba was able to get us some plump and luscious mangoes which were perfect for Bender's dessert of Mango with Chili and Lime Sugar.

Pearls, pearl shells, and pearling have always been a part of the way of life in Broome. In fact, Baamba told us how in his dad's day the kids used to use found pearls as marbles!

Baamba arranged for us to go out and see how pearls are grown and harvested. We were whisked away by chopper along the glorious coastline to the Willie Creek Pearl Farm. Pearl farms are not as exotic as they sound. Basically, they are line after line of pearl shells suspended in the ocean from a rope, filtering the clean waters of the north-west, growing big and fat, and growing South Sea pearls that have been seeded inside. It's a long slow process, and the shells need to be pulled from the water every eight weeks or so, and cleaned to avoid diseases. South Sea pearls are known as the 'queen of pearls', and Broome pearls are sold around the world. While the traditional Japanese oyster pearl produces pearls about 1/2 inch (11 millimetres) in diameter, the larger South Sea pearls native to Australia can grow up to 3/4 inch (18 millimetres) and even, rarely, up to almost an inch (21 millimetres)!

In the early days — the days of brass helmets, and hand bellows — diving for pearls was a very dangerous job indeed. A walk in the local cemetery is proof of that. More than 600 Japanese alone, among the people of many nationalities drawn to Broome to work as divers, lost their lives on the job. In 1910, Broome was the pearling capital of the world. This first industry was based around pearl shell (mother of pearl), which was in demand for buttons, cutlery handles, walking stick handles, and as inlay in swords and pistols. But in 1958, the advent of the plastic button virtually wiped out the industry.

We, however, were here for the pearl meat. This is very rare and, at around $50 a pound (500 grams), is likely to stay at the curiosity end of the gastronomic table. The texture is fine, the colour light grey, and, as we later find out, the meat tastes like a cross between abalone and scallop. It's not everyone's cup of tea and, personally, I'll stick to scallops, but it was fun.

Now we have our ingredients, let's get cooking.

Tian of mud crab, avocado, and tomato with lime mayonnaise

This is a perfect dish to prepare if you are out to impress. It's quite a formal dish, and one that takes a little more time than most; however, it looks very impressive. If you are after a more casual approach, use all the same ingredients and make a salad instead — this way you will cut down your prep time but will still have the same great taste.

SERVES 4

Poaching liquid

16 cups	water	4 L
1	carrot, cut into chunks	1
2	celery stalks, sliced into lengths	2
1	head garlic, unpeeled, roughly chopped	1
1	leek, cut into chunks	1
1	onion, chopped	1
8	white peppercorns	8
2	fresh bay leaves	2
1	sprig fresh thyme	

1	live mud crab (any large crab will do), weighing about 3 lb (1.5 kg)	1
8	large beefsteak tomatoes, weighing about 8 oz (250 g)	8
20	fresh coriander leaves	20
2 tbsp	freshly squeezed lime juice	30 mL
2	ripe avocados, finely diced	2
1	bird's-eye chili, deseeded and finely chopped	1
1 tsp	olive oil	5 mL
6 tbsp	lime mayonnaise (see recipe page 64)	90 mL
1 tsp	tomato paste	5 mL
1/4 cup	mayonnaise	50 mL
	Sea salt	

1 Place all the poaching ingredients in a large saucepan, and bring to the boil. Reduce heat to low, and simmer for 10 minutes. Add the crab, and cut off the string, releasing the claws. Cook for 18–20 minutes. Drain, and chill the crab, still in its shell, in the refrigerator.

2 Bring a large saucepan of water to the boil. Core the tomatoes, and cut a cross on their tops. Blanch for 10–12 seconds. Refresh in ice cold water, and peel. Using a sharp knife, cut the outer flesh off the heart of each tomato in one piece; it needs to be at least 3 inches (8 cm) wide. Lie out flat, and cut out a circle 3 inches (8 cm) in diameter. Repeat with the remaining tomatoes.

3 When the crab is cold, extract all the white meat, ensuring that it is free of any shell. Place the meat in a bowl with the coriander leaves and half the lime juice. In another bowl, combine the avocados, chili and the remaining lime juice.

continued over...

Curtis Stone

4 On a work surface, place a tomato circle inside a 3-inch (8 cm) cookie cutter with high sides. Spoon a quarter of the avocado mixture into the cutter, smoothing the top with the back of a spoon. Place a quarter of the crab mixture on top and smooth the surface. Top with another tomato disc and brush with oil. Spoon a quarter of the lime mayonnaise in the centre of a serving plate and smooth it into a circle. Using a palette knife, place the tian in the centre of the mayonnaise. Gently remove the cutter, leaving the tian in shape. Repeat this procedure until all the tomato, avocado and crab mixture is used.

5 Combine the tomato paste and mayonnaise in a bowl, and stir well. Spoon the tomato mayonnaise into a squeeze bottle, and decorate the plate around the lime mayonnaise with dots of colour. Sprinkle the top of the tian with a little sea salt.

Lime mayonnaise*

1	*free-range egg yolk*	1	
1 tsp	*Dijon mustard*	*5 mL*	
1 tsp	*white wine vinegar*	*5 mL*	
1 tsp	*freshly squeezed lime juice*	*5mL*	
¹/₂ cup	*peanut oil*	*125 mL*	
	Salt and freshly ground white pepper		

1 Place the egg yolk, mustard, vinegar, and lime juice in a mini food processor, and mix until smooth. With the motor running, slowly add the oil in a thin trickle to give a thick mayonnaise. If necessary, incorporate a little warm water at the end to give the right consistency. Season to taste with salt and pepper.

This recipe can be increased by up to four times without jeopardising the balance.

Curtis Stone

Barbecued pearl meat with agrodolce dressing, and a mint and eggplant salad

Agrodolce is Italian for sweet and sour. I prepare this recipe with scallops in my restaurant in London — from what I remember, pearl meat is similar.

SERVES 4

Dressing

2 oz	fresh bread crumbs	60 g
1 oz	blanched almonds	30 g
1	anchovy fillet	1
2 tbsp	freshly squeezed orange juice	30 mL
2 tsp	instant dissolving sugar	10 mL
1/2 oz	bitter dark chocolate (100% cocoa solids), roughly chopped	15 g
1/3 cup	white wine vinegar	75 mL
1/2 cup	water	125 mL
	Salt and freshly ground black pepper	
2 tsp	olive oil	10 mL

Salad

2	small eggplant, thinly sliced	2
7 fl oz	olive oil for shallow frying	200 mL
1 cup	loosely packed fresh mint leaves, torn if large	250 mL
1 tsp	freshly squeezed lemon juice	5 mL
	Extra 2 tsp olive oil	10 mL
11 1/2 oz	pearl meat, or fresh scallops, shrimp or squid	320 g

1 To make the dressing, toast the bread crumbs and almonds in a dry skillet until golden. Pound together using a mortar and pestle, or grind in a small food processor, until fine. Put to one side. Grind the anchovy, orange juice, sugar, and chocolate until paste-like. Bring the vinegar and water to the boil in a small saucepan. Stir in the bread crumb mixture, followed by the anchovy mixture. Reduce the heat, and simmer for 5 minutes. Taste for seasoning, and cool. Stir in the olive oil. It should be a loose dressing.

2 To make the salad, shallow-fry the eggplant in the oil until golden and crisp. Drain on paper towels. Toss with the mint, lemon juice and extra olive oil.

3 Preheat the barbecue. Grill the pearl meat for 20–30 seconds, until just done. Divide the eggplant and mint salad between 4 serving plates, and arrange the grilled pearl meat on top. Drizzle over the dressing, and tuck in.

Ben O'Donoghue

Mud crab and green papaya salad

This is a Thai-influenced salad, so it's not exactly original. David Thompson may give me a hiding for this effort—so please forgive me, David.

SERVES 4

3 lb	live large mud crab (any large crab will do)	1.5 kg

Dressing

2	cloves garlic	2
1/4 tsp	salt	1 mL
4 tsp	dried shrimp*	20 mL
3–5	bird's-eye chilies, seeded	3–5
2 tbsp	palm sugar (jaggery)*	30 mL
3 tbsp	freshly squeezed lime juice	45 mL
2 tbsp	tamarind pulp	30 mL
2–3 tbsp	fish sauce	30–45 mL
1	green papaya or under-ripe honeydew melon, peeled and finely sliced	1
2 tbsp	fresh mint leaves	30 mL
1/4 cup	fresh Thai basil leaves	50 mL
2 tbsp	fresh coriander leaves	30 mL
2	fresh kaffir lime leaves, shredded	2
1	lemongrass stalk, trimmed and finely sliced across the stem	1

1. Place the crab in a large saucepan of cold salted water. Remove the claw ties, so its muscles can relax. Cover, and bring to the boil. Cook at a very low simmer for 20–25 minutes, then transfer to a sink full of ice water to cool quickly.

2. Using a heavy, sharp knife or poultry shears, remove the top shell. Pick all the white meat from the body and legs, making sure that no shell is included. Reserve crabmeat for the salad.

3. To make the dressing, pound the garlic, salt and dried shrimp in a mortar and pestle or a small food processor. Add the chillies, and pound until paste-like. Add the palm sugar, lime juice and tamarind pulp, and blend well. Add enough fish sauce to give a hot, sweet, and sharp dressing, that is balanced at the same time.

4. Place the papaya or honeydew melon in a bowl. Add the reserved white crabmeat, the mint, basil, coriander, kaffir lime leaves, and lemongrass. To serve, add the dressing, and toss lightly.

* Available at specialist Asian food shops.

Zuppa di baccalà

This classic soup from Venice can be as simple or complicated as you like. If you are pressed for time, you can buy the salt cod from a quality Italian delicatessen*. By salting the cod you are drawing out the moisture and intensifying the flavour.

SERVES 6–8

2 lb	salt cod*	1 kg
4 tsp	olive oil	20 mL
8 oz	leeks, white part only, thickly sliced	250 g
	Finely grated rind of 1 orange	
1	sprig fresh thyme	1
5 cups	fish stock	1.25 L
7 fl oz	water	200 mL
8 oz	potatoes, peeled and cubed	250 g
2 cups	35% whipping cream	500 mL
	Freshly ground black pepper	
	Finely chopped fresh chives to garnish	

❶ Soak the cod in cold water for 2–3 hours. Drain, and cover with fresh cold water. Continue in this way, changing the water often, for at least 24 hours. Remove the skin from the fish, and dice the flesh. Heat the olive oil in a large saucepan, and fry the cod over medium heat for 5 minutes. Add the leeks, rind and thyme, and cook over low heat, without browning, for 5 minutes. Add the stock and water, and bring to the boil. Add the potatoes, and simmer for 10–15 minutes, until tender.

❷ Remove from the heat, and allow to cool slightly. Transfer to a food processor, and blend until smooth. Place a fine sieve over a clean saucepan, and strain the soup. Don't discard the solids collected in the sieve: they should resemble a light purée or brandade and will be used to make quenelles. Transfer the fish purée to a bowl, cover, and refrigerate.

❸ Add the cream to the soup, and bring to a simmer. Season to taste with pepper.

❹ Remove the fish purée from the refrigerator. To make the quenelles, using lightly moistened spoons, form a tablespoonful of the purée into an egg shape. Repeat until all the purée is used.

❺ To serve, ladle the soup into bowls. Divide the quenelles between the bowls, and garnish with a sprinkling of chives.

* *It is best to prepare your own salt cod at home. Take a 2-lb (1-kg) fillet of fresh cod, and cover with rock salt. Leave in the refrigerator for 12 hours, then wash off the salt under rapidly running water for 30 minutes.*

Curtis Stone

Barbecued king shrimp skewers wrapped in prosciutto with mango and chili

Being an Aussie I feel proud to say that we have the best shrimp in the world. I have some really fond memories of shrimp, whether it is eating them in a swanky restaurant in Melbourne or straight from a plastic bag on a pier, after buying some from a fish cooperative on the beach. Here is a simple take on how to throw another shrimp on the barbie.

SERVES 4

16	green king shrimp	16
1	large just-ripe mango	1
8	thin slices prosciutto, sliced into halves lengthways	8
¼ cup	chili oil	50 mL
2	lemons, quartered	2

1. Soak 4 wooden skewers in water for 20 minutes. Peel and devein the shrimp, leaving the tail and head intact. Peel the mango, and cut the flesh into 1-inch (2.5-cm) cubes. Place 1 piece of mango in the centre of each shrimp, then wrap a slice of prosciutto around each shrimp.

2. Preheat the barbecue or grill. Thread a shrimp onto a skewer, starting at the tail and coming out close to the head. Add 3 more shrimp to the skewer in this way. Brush with the chili oil. Repeat using the remaining skewers. Char-grill for 1 minute on each side. Squeeze lemon juice over the top, remove from the barbecue, and serve.

Curtis Stone

Thai-style baby barramundi with wok-tossed noodles and greens

Barramundi is a variety of perch, so if you are not lucky enough to get your hands on some barra you can easily substitute perch. Deep-frying fish is a quick hassle-free way to cook — and it is not necessary to have a deep-fryer: you can use a wok or a large saucepan.

SERVES 4

Marinade

2	shallots, finely chopped	2
3	cloves garlic, minced	3
2 tbsp	peeled and minced fresh ginger	30 mL
1	small red chili, deseeded and finely chopped	1
2 tsp	finely chopped fresh mint	10 mL
2 tsp	finely chopped fresh basil	10 mL
2 tsp	finely chopped fresh coriander	10 mL
1	fresh lemongrass stalk, trimmed and finely chopped	1
1 tbsp	light soy sauce	15 mL
4	baby barramundi fillets, weighing about 7 oz (200 g), cut into 2 or 3 thin slices*	4
1	head broccoli, weighing about 5 oz (150 g)	1
7 oz	hokkien noodles	200 g
3 cups	vegetable oil for deep-frying (approx)	750 mL
4 oz	cornflour	125 g
2	shallots, sliced	2
2	carrots, peeled, canaled** and sliced	2
2	baby bok choy, halved lengthways	2
1/4 cup	light soy sauce	50 mL
4 tsp	sweet chili sauce	20 mL
1/2 cup	loosely packed fresh coriander leaves to serve	125 mL

① Combine all the marinade ingredients in a bowl, and mix well. Add the fish fillets, and marinate for 15 minutes at room temperature. Slice the broccoli stem thinly, and reserve. Trim the head into 12 florets. Bring a large saucepan of salted water to the boil. Blanch the florets for 2–3 minutes. Remove with a slotted spoon, and reserve. Drop the noodles into the boiling water, and cook for about 45 seconds, until softened. Drain well.

② Put 2 tsp (10 mL) oil into a wok. Pour the remainder into a deep-fryer or a large heavy-based saucepan. Heat to a point where a cube of bread, when dropped in, browns in 15 seconds. Drain the marinated fish, pat dry with paper towel, and dust in the cornflour. Deep-fry in batches for 2–3 minutes, until golden, and drain on paper towels.

③ Meanwhile, heat the oil in the wok and fry the broccoli slices, shallots, and carrots for 15–20 seconds. Add the bok choy, and when wilted, add the noodles, soy sauce, and sweet chili sauce. Gently toss until heated through. Moisten with a little water, if needed.

continued over...

Curtis Stone

Thai-style baby barramundi with wok-tossed noodles and greens, continued...

④ Neatly pile the noodle and vegetable mixture in the centre of 4 serving bowls. Place 2 or 3 barramundi slices on top, and arrange 3 broccoli florets around the edge of each. Sprinkle with coriander, and serve at once.

* *Why not get the fishmonger to do this when you buy the fish.*
** *To canal the carrots, cut out troughs along their length, right around the perimeter.*

Curtis Stone

Mango with chili and lime sugar

This interesting combination of hot, sweet and sour is common in Asian cooking. It's dead simple to prepare and it's a great way to finish a meal.

SERVES 4

4	ripe mangoes, peeled and sliced	4
2–3	dried bird's-eye chilies	2–3
2 tbsp	instant dissolving sugar	30 mL
	Finely grated rind of 2 limes	

1. Arrange the mango slices on a plate. Place the chilies and a little of the sugar in a mortar, and pound to break up the chili. Add the remaining sugar and the rind, and pound to incorporate.

2. Sprinkle the chili mixture over the mango slices, or serve separately on the side for guests to help themselves.

Ben O'Donoghue

Pineapple and black pepper tarte Tatin

Tarte Tatin was invented in France at the beginning of the twentieth century by the Tatin sisters, and was served at Maxim's in Paris, where it is now a permanent fixture on the menu. It is classically made with apples, but pineapple also works well. The tarte takes a little bit of time to prepare, but it can be made well in advance, and is easy to serve.

MAKES 1 TART

4 tbsp	unsalted butter, softened	60 mL
4 tbsp	instant dissolving sugar	60 mL
1/2 tsp	coarsely ground black pepper	2 mL
1 x 2-inch	thick slice of pineapple, cored	5-cm
2 oz	pre-rolled puff pastry	60 g
	Good-quality vanilla ice cream to serve	

1 Grease the base of a small blini pan* with the butter. Sprinkle the sugar on top.

2 Press the black pepper onto 1 side of the pineapple, and place, pepper-side down, on the sugar. Cut the pastry into a circle 1 inch (2.5 cm) larger than the diameter of the pan. Place over the pineapple, and tuck the edges down between the pan and the pineapple. Rest for 10 minutes.

3 Preheat the oven to 375°F (190°C). Place the pan over a low heat for 3–5 minutes, until you see the sugar bubble up, and start to colour, and turn light brown around the side of the pastry. Transfer to the oven, and bake for 30 minutes. Remove and rest for 10 minutes, then invert the pan onto a clean plate.

4 Serve with vanilla ice cream.

* Blini pans approximately 4 inches (10 cm) in diameter and at least 2 inches (5 cm) deep are useful not just for this tart and for making blini, but for making small pancakes, Yorkshire puddings, and perfect fried eggs.

Curtis Stone

Banana, pecan, and walnut hotcakes

I love the odd banana and some fantastic organic bananas are grown in Broome.

SERVES 6

1¹/₂ cups	all-purpose flour	375 mL
1 tbsp	baking powder	15 mL
1 tbsp	instant dissolving sugar	15 mL
2 oz	chopped walnuts and pecan nuts	60 g
6	ripe bananas	6
1	large free-range egg	1
1 cup	milk	250 mL
2 tbsp	dark rum	30 mL
6 tbsp	butter, softened	90 mL
	35% whipping cream to serve	
	Golden syrup to serve	

1 Sift the flour into a bowl, and add the baking powder, sugar, and half the nuts. Mash 3 of the bananas in another bowl. Add the egg, milk, rum and half the butter, mix well, and add to the dry ingredients. Stir well to combine.

2 Grease a large non-stick skillet with a little of the remaining butter. Spoon 2 tbsp (30 mL) batter into the pan to give a hotcake about 3 inches (8 cm) in diameter — 3 hotcakes at a time fit comfortably. Cook over medium heat until bubbles appear on the surface, and the underside is golden brown. Flip over, and cook for a further 1–2 minutes. Remove from the pan, and keep warm. Continue in this way until all the batter and butter are used.

3 Slice the 3 remaining bananas, and serve with the hotcakes, cream, a drizzle of golden syrup, and the remaining nuts sprinkled over the top.

Ben O'Donoghue

Banana semifreddo

This is one of my favourite recipes using banana.

SERVES 4–6

10	free-range egg yolks	10
3½ fl oz	warmed honey	100 mL
3 tbsp	rum or banana liqueur	45mL
4 tbsp	instant dissolving sugar	60 mL
3	large ripe bananas	3
5	egg whites	5
2 cups	18% cream	500 mL
7 oz	dark chocolate (70% cocoa solids), chopped	200 g
2 oz	unsalted roasted peanuts (other nuts may be used), finely chopped	60 g

❶ Line a 10- x 6-inch (25- x 15-cm) loaf pan or a glass pudding bowl with plastic wrap and place in the freezer to chill.

❶ Place the egg yolks in a bowl with the honey, rum, and half the sugar. Place the bowl over a saucepan of simmering water, and whisk until the mixture is light, fluffy, and doubled in volume.

❶ Mash the bananas with a fork in a large bowl. Add the egg mixture, and stir to combine. In a clean bowl, whisk the egg whites with the remaining sugar until stiff. Fold into the banana mixture. Whip the cream to soft peaks, and fold into the banana mixture. Fold in half the chocolate, spoon into the prepared pan or bowl, and freeze until set.

❶ Melt the remaining chocolate by placing it in a heatproof bowl over a saucepan of simmering water (don't let the bowl touch the water), or in a microwave oven. Unmould the semifreddo onto a serving plate. Using a spoon, drizzle half the melted chocolate over the top in a criss-cross pattern, then sprinkle with the peanuts. Drizzle the remaining chocolate over the top. Return to the freezer until required.

❶ About 15–20 minutes before serving, transfer to the refrigerator to soften.

Hunter Valley

Hunter Valley

Big Cellars, Balloons, and Barrington Tops

Curtis Stone

The Hunter Valley is well known in Australia as a premium wine-growing area. The valley, being almost 125 miles (200 kilometres) in length, has an amazing array of agricultural produce, which is what drew us to have a look around.

My first impressions of the Hunter Valley were just how lush, green, and delightful the scenery was. In places, it looks like parts of Wales, in others, like parts of Canada, yet it is all distinctly Australian: from the depth of colour in the sky, and the unique purple colour of the distant hills to the laconic, dry humour of the country folk. Our journey took us the entire length of the Hunter, from Cessnock in the east to the spectacular Barrington Tops in the north-west. In some places it took us back in time, and in others it showed us what the future in food could be.

The passion and dedication of the producers we were lucky to meet was apparent. With these people at the helm, it's my opinion that the Hunter Valley will continue to grow and develop its reputation as a quality producer of wine, beef, lamb, cheese, goats, native fish, rabbits, mushrooms, game birds, and poultry.

While back in London, I had seen some photographs of the Hunter region that were taken from a hot-air balloon. I thought this sounded brilliant, so I set the alarm one morning for 4.30, spent ten minutes banging on Bender's door to wake him (he's not exactly a light sleeper), and then we headed off to Cessnock airport. It was still dark at 5.30 am when we got there, but one small office had its light burning brightly, and a number of other would-be aviators had already gathered outside. Ballooning sure is popular here, there were three flights going up that morning — in our balloon there were twelve passengers. They pack 'em in like they do on the London Underground.

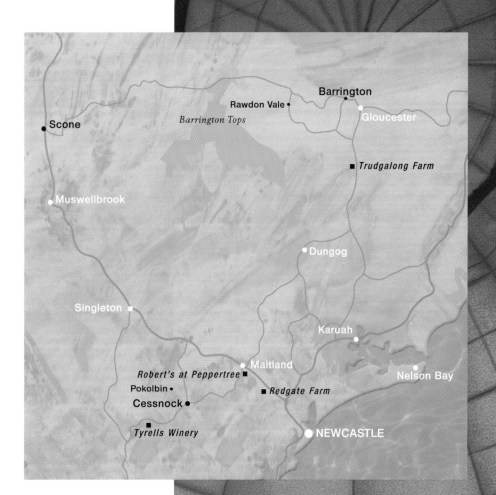

Scone

Barrington

Rawdon Vale

Barrington Tops

Gloucester

Trudgalong Farm

Muswellbrook

Dungog

Singleton

Karuah

Maitland

Robert's at Peppertree

Nelson Bay

Pokolbin

Redgate Farm

Cessnock

NEWCASTLE

Tyrells Winery

Ballooning was not exactly as I had expected. From the filling of the balloon on its side to the roar of the gas flame, and the cavernous space of hot air, it was an experience and a half. When we were aloft, the view was spectacular. We drifted gently and peacefully (except for the occasional burst of the gas flame) over row after row of vines, across cattle-filled paddocks, and over creeks and bushland. The landing was a little bumpier than I'd anticipated, but it must have been a regular occurrence for the cattle in our landing paddock merely ambled away as we approached. Breakfast at 7.30 am was well received, and we wolfed down a huge plate of bacon and eggs. After all, we'd already been up for hours!

Our next stop was Redgate Farm where we were greeted by a quacking flock of plump ducks. Inside there were quite a few recently hatched fluffy ducklings, and thousands upon thousands of quails. I think quails are quite finicky on the prep side, but boy, do they taste good. So that's what we chose.

Another stop was Trudgalong Farm, built on a dramatic rocky ridge overlooking its paddocks. Here chickens roamed freely, ducklings puddled near the dam, and in the bottom paddock was a flock of very contented goats. These goats are bred for the Sydney markets, and for selected restaurants. Goat, or kid, is one of my favourite meats because of its rich taste. As well, the dams on the property are stocked with native silver perch, which are also specially bred and marketed. I was sent out with a fishing rod, and some bait (and Bender's sceptical good wishes), and had a lucky catch. These perch are beautiful eating, and similar in look to barramundi. Their natural environment is the safety of muddy water, so growers often put their fish into clear water for some days to purge them of their slightly muddy taste before market.

Barrington Tops is a World Heritage Wilderness area but is surrounded by some of Australia's finest grazing land, and watered by cool pristine mountain streams. Taking the road towards Scone, we wound our way through a beautiful steep-sided valley, and then abruptly turned upwards, heading towards the clouds. On the way down the other side of the rise, the vegetation became distinctly rainforest in nature. Giant tree ferns lined the roadside and vines hung from tall trees.

We headed towards Rawdon Vale and to Stobo House, an extraordinary old place built room by room over the years from stones found on the property. Here, in this pristine environment, they breed wonderful aged beef for the restaurant table. As we arrived, they were about to head out to bring in a mob of cattle. It was great to be back on a horse after quite a few years. Bender, on the other hand … well, looking at his style, I think from now on I'll call him Bob.

Grapes have been grown, and wine produced in the Hunter since the 1830s. One of the earliest wineries was Tyrrell's, which was established in 1858. We visited, and were lucky enough to get an insight into Australia's remarkable success in international wine exports from Bruce Tyrell, fourth-generation winemaker and voice of the Hunter wine region. Bruce took us into the oldest section of the winery. Old log beams hold up the ceiling, an ancient wine press stands idly in one corner, and row after row of old, large, dusty barrels sit on a hardened earth floor. The floor is sprayed with water every evening to keep the humidity up and the dust down.

By the main winery is the original slab-sided wooden hut that served as the Tyrrell pioneers' first home in the Hunter almost 150 years ago. The land was considered poor for pasture but great wines have come from the soils of this hilly property.

With the produce we had collected we held a luncheon in the gardens of Robert Molines' restaurant at Peppertree vineyard. Robert is originally from the south of France, born in the hills above Monaco. A great advocate of fresh, local produce, his training is from the classical French tradition, so I immediately felt at home in his kitchen. We ate at a table set on the lush lawn between a row of topiaried trees. An autumnal vineyard, and a babbling brook next to a sweet white chapel completed the idyllic scene.

Silver perch en papillote with braised romaine lettuce

SERVES 4

Braised lettuce

1 tbsp	olive oil	15 mL
1	carrot, finely chopped	1
1	onion, finely chopped	1
1	celery stalk, finely chopped	1
1/4 cup	red wine	50 mL
2	baby romaine lettuce	2
2 cups	veal stock	500 mL
2	fresh bay leaves	2
2	sprigs thyme	2
10	black peppercorns	10
4	fillets silver perch (or use sea bass or bream), weighing about 7 oz (200 g)	4
1	carrot, cut into julienne	1
1	small bulb fennel, cut into julienne	1
1	shallot, finely sliced	1
1	leek, white part only, cut into julienne	1
3 tbsp	dry vermouth, such as Noilly Prat	45 mL
3 tbsp	fish stock	45 mL
	Salt and freshly ground white pepper	
	Sprigs fresh flat-leaf parsley to garnish	

1. To braise the lettuce, preheat the oven to 400°F (200°C). Heat the olive oil in a roasting pan over medium heat, add the carrot, onion and celery, and cook until softened. Deglaze the pan with the wine. Cut the lettuces in half lengthways, and place in the pan cut side down on top of the vegetables. Add the veal stock, bay leaves, thyme, and peppercorns. Cover the pan with foil, and put in the oven for 25–30 minutes, until soft.

2. While the lettuce is in the oven, for each fish parcel take a piece of foil approximately 12 inches (30 cm) square, and place the julienne of carrot, fennel, shallot, and leek in the centre. Put a fish fillet on top, and drizzle over some vermouth and fish stock. Season with salt and pepper.

3. Fold the edges of the foil over the fish to form a tightly sealed parcel in the shape of a large pasty. Then put the foil parcels in a large ovenproof skillet over high heat. The liquid inside the parcels will begin to boil, causing steam to expand the parcels. When the parcels have reached this stage, transfer the skillet to the oven and cook for a further 4–6 minutes.

4. Once the lettuce is soft, remove from the roasting pan. Strain and reserve the liquid. Place half a lettuce in the centre of each serving plate.

5. Remove the foil parcels from the oven and open them, being careful not to burn yourself on the steam. Place the fish on the lettuce and garnish with the vegetable julienne. Sauce with a little of the reserved liquid and garnish with a sprig of parsley.

Curtis Stone

Poached perch with garlic, ginger, and green onions

The farming of fish is an important part of a sustainable fishing resource that supplies both professional and domestic chefs. The important thing is that these aqua farmers produce their fish in the least intensive manner possible, and re-create the fish's natural diet. In this way the final product is healthy, and as close as possible to the qualities of a wild fish. At the fish farm we visited in the Hunter Valley this ethical approach was in practise and the results were in the tasting — bloody fantastic.

SERVES 4

Poaching liquor

3½ oz	fresh ginger	100 g
8 cups	water	2 L
10	green onions, white part only	10
2 tbsp	salt	30 mL
⅓ cup	rice wine vinegar	75 mL
4	silver perch (or use sea bass or bream), weighing about 14 oz 400 g, cleaned	4

Dressing

2–3	cloves garlic, peeled	2–3
	Salt	
⅓ cup	rice wine vinegar (approx)	75 mL
⅓ cup	peanut oil (approx)	75 mL
4 tbsp	light soy sauce	60 mL
10	green onions, green tops only, finely sliced	10

1. To make the poaching liquor, peel and grate the ginger, and place the ginger trimmings in a stockpot. Reserve the grated ginger for the dressing. Add the water, green onions, salt and vinegar, and bring to the boil. Strain into a fish-poaching kettle or a baking pan large enough to take the perch side by side.

2. Place on a low heat and keep just under simmering point. Lower the fish into the poaching liquor so that they are completely covered. Leave to cook gently for 15 minutes. They are done when a spine from the dorsal fin pulls out easily.

3. Meanwhile, make the dressing by placing the garlic and reserved grated ginger into a mortar. Add a pinch of salt and pound to a paste. Add enough vinegar and oil to make a dressing. This step can also be done in a mini food processor.

4. Transfer the fish to warm serving plates. Drizzle the soy sauce over the top, followed by a little poaching liquor. Spoon the dressing over the fish and scatter over the sliced spring onion tops.

5. Serve with steamed rice.

Char sui pork with Asian vegetables

Char sui translates to barbecue pork and is a Cantonese specialty. The marinade is very easy to knock out. Not only can you use a fillet as I have done here, but anything from ribs to pork belly is suitable.

SERVES 4

Marinade

7 fl oz	char sui paste*	200 mL
1 tbsp	soy sauce	15 mL
3 tbsp	honey	45 mL
1	clove garlic, bruised	1
1/2-inch	piece fresh ginger, peeled and sliced	1-cm
2	medium pork fillets	2

Vegetables

8 oz	broccoli	250 g
1	zucchini	1
1	carrot	1
1/4	red bell pepper	1/4
1/4	yellow bell pepper	1/4
1/4	green bell pepper	1/4
1 tbsp	vegetable oil	15 mL
1	shallot, sliced	1
1	small clove garlic, minced	1
1/4 tsp	peeled and minced fresh ginger	1 mL
1/2	head bok choy, shredded	1/2
2 tbsp	soy sauce	30 mL
1 tbsp	oyster sauce	15 mL
1 tsp	sesame oil	5 mL

1. Combine all the marinade ingredients in a ceramic or glass bowl, mix well, and add the pork fillets, turning to coat. Cover with plastic wrap and marinate for 24 hours in the refrigerator.

2. Preheat the oven to 350°F (180°C).

3. Remove the pork from the marinade, and seal on all sides in a medium skillet, 5–6 minutes. Transfer to a roasting pan, and place in the oven for 8 minutes. Remove and rest, covered with foil, for 3–4 minutes.

4. Cut the broccoli, zucchini, carrot and bell peppers into bite-size pieces. Heat the oil in a wok, and add the cut vegetables along with the shallot, garlic, ginger and bok choy. Stir-fry for 15–20 seconds. Add the soy sauce and oyster sauce, and continue frying until the vegetables are al dente, 20–30 seconds. Stir through the sesame oil. Transfer the vegetables to serving bowls.

5. Carve the pork diagonally into 1/2-inch (1-cm) slices and arrange on top of the vegetables. Drizzle any juices from the roasting pan over the top and serve.

Available from Asian specialty food shops

Curtis Stone

Grilled quail salad with speck, radicchio, red onion, and lentils

SERVES 4

3¹/₂ oz	puy lentils*, rinsed	100 g
1	celery stalk, cut into 3 lengths	1
4	celery leaves	4
2	cloves garlic, peeled	2
2 tbsp	freshly squeezed lemon juice	30 mL
3–4 tbsp	extra-virgin olive oil	45–60 mL
	Salt and freshly ground black pepper	
1	medium red onion, peeled and sliced into ¹/₄-inch (5-mm) rings	1
3–4 tsp	balsamic vinegar	15–20 mL
¹/₄	head radicchio, cut into thin wedges	¹/₄
16	large quails**	16
2 tsp	fresh thyme leaves	10 mL
8	thin slices speck	8
¹/₂ cup	fresh mint leaves	125 mL
¹/₂ cup	picked watercress leaves	125 mL
1–2 tbsp	aged balsamic vinegar***	15–30 mL

1 Place the lentils in a saucepan, and cover with cold water to a depth twice their volume. Tie the celery stalks and leaves together, and add to the water along with the garlic. Bring to the boil and simmer for 40 minutes, until the lentils are tender. Discard the celery and garlic, and strain. Place lentils in a bowl, add the lemon juice and 1 tbsp (15 mL) oil, and season with salt and pepper. Set aside, and keep warm.

2 Heat a griddle plate to medium and brush with olive oil. Cook the onion rings slowly so they become soft and sweet. Transfer to a bowl, and toss with 1 tsp (5 mL) olive oil and 1 tsp (5 mL) balsamic vinegar. Brush the griddle with a little more oil, and slowly cook the radicchio wedges until lightly browned. Season, and add to the bowl with the onion. Keep warm.

3 Preheat the oven to 350ºF (180ºC). Season the quails with salt, pepper and thyme. Heat a skillet to hot, add a little oil, and quickly brown the quails and speck. Transfer to a roasting pan, and roast for 10 minutes. Remove from the oven, and drizzle with a little oil and balsamic vinegar.

continued over...

* Where puy lentils are unavailable, use green lentils.
** If you're in luck, your butcher or poulterer might partially bone the quail. Otherwise, cut them in half lengthways.
*** If aged balsamic vinegar is too expensive, you can gently reduce normal balsamic in a small pan until thick, then allow to cool.

Ben O'Donoghue

4 Adjust the seasoning of the onion and radicchio mixture if required, then divide between 4 plates. Spoon the lentils onto each plate, place the quails on top, and divide the speck evenly between the servings.

5 In a bowl, mix the mint and watercress leaves with the juices from the roasting pan. Spoon over the top of the quails. To serve, drizzle a ring of aged balsamic around the salad and a trickle of oil.

Ben O'Donoghue

Spiced loin of lamb with spinach and pine nuts

This is a different way of using spices. You are making your own curry paste and then infusing the food rather than overpowering the flavours. When using strong-flavoured ingredients I always prefer to control the amount.

SERVES 6–8

Sauce

1 tbsp	grape seed oil (or use vegetable, sunflower or rape seed oil)	15 mL
4 lb	diced lamb (from the shoulder)	2 kg
2	shallots, peeled and halved	2
8	sprigs fresh thyme	8
4	sprigs fresh rosemary	4
Pinch	saffron	
2	star anise	2
10 cups	lamb or beef stock	2.5 L
4 tsp	pine nuts	20 mL

Curry-infused oil

4 tsp	cumin seeds	20 mL
2 tbsp	coriander seeds	30 mL
1 tbsp	fennel seeds	20 mL
1 tbsp	ground turmeric	20 mL
4 tsp	paprika	20 mL
2 tbsp	grape seed oil (or use vegetable, sunflower or rape seed oil)	30 mL
2 tbsp	butter	30 mL
5 oz	baby spinach leaves, washed	150g
2	rolled and boned lamb loins, weighing about 1½ lb (750 g)	2

1. To make the sauce, heat the oil to very hot in a large heavy-based saucepan. Fry the diced lamb in 3–4 batches over high heat for 5–6 minutes, until golden brown. Add the shallots, thyme, rosemary, saffron, star anise and stock, and bring to the boil. Cook at a rolling boil, skimming often, until the liquid is reduced by half, about 1 hour. Strain into a smaller saucepan. Reserve the diced lamb for later use. Bring the sauce back to the boil and reduce by half again, 15–20 minutes. Add the pine nuts.

2. In the meantime, make the curry-infused oil. Toast the cumin seeds, coriander seeds and fennel seeds in a dry skillet for 3–4 minutes, until aromatic. Transfer to a mortar and pestle, add the turmeric and paprika, and crush to a fine paste. This step can be done using a spice mill. Transfer to a small bowl and stir in the oil. Brush all over the lamb and set aside.

3. Preheat the oven to 400°F (200°C).

continued opposite...

Curtis Stone

4. Heat a large saucepan to very hot, and add the butter and spinach all at once. Toss to coat the spinach, and remove from the heat once wilted. Strain off any excess liquid, and return to the pan to keep warm.

5. Brown the lamb all over in a hot skillet. Transfer to a roasting pan, and roast for 6 minutes for rare, 8 minutes for medium rare. Remove from the oven, cover with foil, and rest for 3–4 minutes. Slice.

6. To serve, place the spinach in the centre of serving plates, and arrange some lamb slices on top. Drizzle the sauce around the outside and serve.

Porterhouse pot-roasted with bay, garlic, and red wine vinegar

This dish would be great with a lovely creamy purée of parsnips or some braised silver beet or Swiss chard.

SERVES 4–6

2 lb	porterhouse steak	1 kg
	Salt and freshly ground black pepper	
2 tbsp	olive oil for browning	30 mL
1/4 cup	butter	50 mL
10	fresh bay leaves	10
4	cloves garlic, peeled and halved	4
1 1/2 cups	Cabernet Sauvignon vinegar	375 mL

1. Trim the fat on the steak to about 1 inch (2.5 cm) thick. Using a sharp knife, cut a crisscross pattern at 1/2-inch (1-cm) intervals across the fat. Season lightly with salt, but add plenty of pepper. Heat the oil in a large heavy-based saucepan. Add the steak and brown on all sides, leaving the fatty side until last. Reduce the heat, and slowly brown the fat; at the same time you will be rendering it (reducing the fat content). Remove the beef from the pan, and drain off the fat.

2. Melt the butter in the saucepan until foaming, then add the steak. Add the bay leaves, garlic and 1/3 cup (75 mL) vinegar. Moisten a piece of waxed paper large enough to cover the pan. Push the damp paper down into the pan to rest on and cover the beef entirely. Simmer over low heat until the vinegar reduces by half. Add a little more vinegar and when that reduces, add some more. Continue in this way until the beef is cooked to medium, 50–70 minutes. The sauce should never completely reduce because you are trying to create an emulsion (a creamy mixture of the beef fat and the vinegar). Add water, if necessary.

3. Turn off the heat, and rest for 10 minutes. Slice the beef, and serve. Spoon a little of the sauce over the beef, and garnish with the bay leaves and garlic.

Ben O'Donoghue

Standing roasted veal rib with a fricassee of cabbage and mushrooms

SERVES 6

1 tbsp	olive oil	15 mL
1	veal rib roast, weighing about 2¾ lb (1.25 kg)	1
	Salt and freshly ground black pepper	
½	Savoy cabbage	½
¼ cup	butter	50 mL
2	cloves garlic, finely chopped	2
7 oz	fresh porcini (or similar wild mushrooms), sliced	200 g
⅓ cup	18% cream	75 mL
2 tsp	chopped fresh chives	10 mL
2 tbsp	finely chopped fresh flat-leaf parsley	30 mL

① Preheat the oven to 400°F (200°C). Heat the oil in a large, heavy-based skillet, and seal the veal over high heat until browned all over, 6–8 minutes. Season with salt and pepper, transfer to a roasting pan and place in the oven for 40 minutes.

② Discard the outer leaves and core of the cabbage, and finely slice the leaves. Bring a large saucepan of lightly salted water to the boil, and blanch the leaves for 2 minutes. Drain, refresh in cold water, and drain well.

③ Melt the butter in a separate saucepan, and sweat the garlic without colouring over low heat for 30 seconds. Add the porcini, and sauté for 2 minutes, then remove from the pan.

④ Add the cabbage to the pan, and cook until al dente, about 2 minutes. Return the mushrooms to the pan, and add the cream. Cook, stirring once or twice, for 2–3 minutes. Stir in the chives and parsley, and season with salt and pepper.

⑤ Remove the veal from the oven, and cover with foil. Rest for 10 minutes. Carve into slices at the table and serve over the cabbage and mushroom fricassee.

Curtis Stone

Chocolate bread and butter pudding

When it comes to English classics, one of my favourite things is the timeless bread and butter pudding. I have fiddled around with it a little and added some chocolate and some Baileys liqueur, which adds a little richness and gives it a lovely texture. I use brioche instead of bread, which already contains a lot of egg and butter, so there is no need to butter the bread. Croissants also work well as a substitute for bread.

SERVES 4

2½ cups	35% whipping cream	625 mL
7 fl oz	Baileys Irish Cream liqueur	200 mL
5 oz	sugar	150 g
2	vanilla beans, split in half lengthways	2
9	free-range egg yolks	9
9	free-range eggs	9
10	slices brioche, each slice about ½-inch (1-cm) thick	10
7 oz	dark chocolate (70% cocoa solids), chopped	200 g

1 Place the cream, Baileys, sugar and vanilla in a large saucepan, and heat, stirring, until the sugar dissolves. Remove from the heat, and cool. Remove the vanilla.

2 Preheat the oven to 250°F (120°C), and grease a shallow 9-inch (1.5-L) oval baking dish. Whisk the egg yolks and eggs together in a large bowl, and strain in the cream mixture. Whisk lightly to blend. Cut the brioche slices in half diagonally, and arrange in the prepared dish in slightly overlapping layers. Pour the cream mixture over the top, and leave for 10 minutes.

3 Melt the chocolate in a microwave oven, or place it in a heatproof bowl over a saucepan of hot water, making sure that the water does not touch the bowl. Pour over the top of the pudding. Place in a baking pan half filled with warm water and transfer to the oven. Bake until set and golden, about 50 minutes.

Curtis Stone

Pears baked in red wine and vanilla

Pears are a fantastic autumn fruit, plus they are cheap and readily available. They are particularly good baked, as a dessert. This recipe is very easy, and looks great. While I was in the Hunter Valley, surrounded by some of the best wine in the country, I thought I'd take the opportunity to try a variation of the classic dessert made with Barolo that I once ate in Piedmont in Italy. Choose pears with a fine skin to ensure a better eating texture.

SERVES 4

4	ripe pears	4
4 tbsp	unsalted butter	60 mL
$3^{1}/_{2}$ oz	instant dissolving sugar	100 g
$1–1^{1}/_{2}$ tbsp	water	15–20 mL
2	vanilla beans, split in half lengthways	2
	Grated rind of $^{1}/_{4}$ orange	
2 cups	red wine, such as Cabernet Sauvignon	500 mL
4 tbsp	crème fraîche	60 mL

1. Preheat the oven to 300°F (150°C).

2. Wash and dry the pears, then cut a small slice from the bottom of each so it can stand upright. Smear the butter all over them, and sprinkle with 2 tbsp (30 mL) sugar.

3. In a heavy-based ovenproof pot large enough to hold the pears upright, combine the remaining sugar with enough water to make a paste. Heat until the sugar paste turns a light golden colour. Add the vanilla, rind and half the red wine. Place the pears upright in the pot and transfer to the oven.

4. Bake, spooning the red wine sauce over the pears at frequent intervals, until the pears are soft and the syrup is reduced, about 45 minutes. Add more wine if the liquid reduces too much.

5. The pears are cooked when the flesh is soft and the outside slightly wrinkled. Remove from the oven, and cool in the pot to room temperature. To serve, drizzle the syrup over the pears and add a spoonful of crème fraîche.

Ben O'Donoghue

White chocolate cheesecake

This is a simple baked cheesecake that is fantastic served with fresh or poached berries. I don't make it with a traditional base, but instead line the tin with cookie crumbs.

SERVES 4–6

2 oz	cookie crumbs made from shortbread or chocolate chip cookies	60 g
1	vanilla bean, split in half lengthways	1
8 oz	white chocolate, chopped	250 g
1 cup	crème fraîche	250 mL
1 lb	cream cheese, softened	500 g
4	large free-range eggs	4

1. Preheat the oven to 300°F (150°C). Grease an 8-inch (2 L) springform pan. Throw in the biscuit crumbs, and roll the pan around to coat the sides. Leave the excess on the base in an even layer.

2. Scrape the seeds from the vanilla bean into a heatproof bowl, and add the white chocolate. Place the bowl over a saucepan of simmering water, don't let the water touch the bowl, until the chocolate melts. Fold in the crème fraîche, and stir until smooth.

3. Beat the cream cheese until soft and smooth. Add the eggs, one at a time, beating well after each addition. Fold in the white chocolate mixture, and stir well. Pour into the prepared pan. Bang the pan down on the bench to remove any air bubbles.

4. Transfer the pan to a baking dish half filled with warm water. Place in the oven, and bake until the cheesecake is firm and golden brown, 50–60 minutes. Don't worry if the top does not colour very much; it is more important that the centre is cooked so that it wobbles, but doesn't crack. Rest for several hours to cool and become firm, then turn out and slice into wedges for serving.

Ben O'Donoghue

New Norcia

New Norcia

Cattle, Goats, and Monks

Curtis Stone

We headed north from Perth along the Great Northern Highway to a monastery town called New Norcia. Bender had played Aussie Rules footy here as a kid so there were no surprises for him, but for me the first encounter was quite startling. In the middle of nowhere, a little piece of Spain appears to have been scooped up and laid out. There's history in every building and artefact. And living history, too, in the sheltered life the monks lead — life that has essentially not changed for centuries.

I'd read that in 1846 a group of Spanish Benedictine monks led by Bishops Rosendo Salvado and José Serra landed in Fremantle, Western Australia, and then walked 112 miles (180 kilometres) north to build a self-sufficient mission and orphanage, which operated until 1973. Spanish Classical, Byzantine, and Gothic buildings with internal court-yards were built in the stifling Australian heat. It's Australia's only monastic town, and this is reflected in the amazing collection of religious art in its gallery.

New Norcia was most likely the site of Australia's first experience with Mediterranean cuisines. The monks' first task was the planting of an olive grove. The oil was used as medicine for wounds and stomach ailments, for hair care, and for holy purposes. Very useful even then! Today, Dom Paulino looks after the olive trees, and also makes the monastery's olive oil in an ancient wheel press driven by whirring gears, and pulleys. Little has changed in his world except that at ninety-three Dom Paulino gets about his grove on a bright yellow four-wheeled farm bike. He's been at the monastery since he left Spain almost seventy-five years ago. For the first fifty years he was the monastery baker. He only ever made one type of bread — a traditional big Spanish four-pounder. He estimates that he has made more than a million loaves in his time, all by hand.

New Norcia is now quite well known for its bakery, so we called in, and met Kingsley Sullivan, who these days not only makes bread for the monks and the town, but has made New Norcia sourdough bread famous, too. The New Norcia Bakery also produces nut cake, pan chocolate, and

Dandaragan • ■ *Noondel*

Moora ○

New Norcia ● ■ *New Norcia Mission*

Grand North Highway

Avon River

Avon Valley ■ *Kervella*

Muchoa ○ Northam ○

• Gidgegannup

York ○

PERTH

FREMANTLE ●

almond biscotti, all of which are sold around the world. The bakery has not changed much in almost 150 years, and there's history in the very bricks themselves. The firebox still glows with logs of hot-burning jarrah, and the brick oven, as big as a small bedroom inside, is the perfect place to bake. Kingsley loves it. And he loves making bread. Broach the subject with him at your peril, lest he never stops talking about it, but that didn't stop me because I love people who are passionate about food and produce.

We asked if we could use the oven to cook in, and Kingsley readily agreed. As it turned out, Ben and I ended up sweating off quite a bit of weight doing it. The temperature in there can reach more than 120°F (50°C) at the height of summer; it's close to hell for those not used to it. The bakers, though, seemed perfectly at home. Once Bender and I were in there cooking, I began to feel there was a kind of link to the wood-oven kitchens of medieval times, and a back-to-basics feeling that was really warming. I mean literally warming, too!

New Norcia was named after the Italian birthplace of St Benedict. Today, on the monastery's 25,000-acre (10,000-hectare) farm, they raise sheep, and produce wheat, canola, grapes, honey, oranges, figs, plums, mandarins, and quinces. Dom Chris, who we'd met earlier, had already promised us a leg of lamb from the monastery's flock of over 5000 sheep, and Kingsley had agreed he'd provide the sourdough bread. Bender said he'd like to cook the lamb with rosemary. As rosemary grows everywhere in New Norcia, a fresh bunch was easy to find near the church.

We called at the orchard behind the monastery, where we met Dom Stephen who gave us some oranges picked fresh from the trees. He suggested we walk down into the cellar, where we met well-known winemaker Nick Humphry. New Norcia also produces that other Mediterranean staple (along with the bread and olives) — wine, both red and white. We found Nick standing among rows of old and dusty barrels. These barrels are the basis of the monastery's solero system, which produces the famous liqueur Muscat that Nick grows and blends. Our 'blind' taste test was a wonderful experience.

During our chat with Kingsley we learnt about other interesting quality produce in the district: Kervella goat cheese and Dandaragan organic beef. That set us off on a quest to visit, and learn more about them.

Gabrielle Kervella was once a violinist in the Western Australian Symphony Orchestra, but now, with her partner, Alan Cockman, she produces a range of award-winning goat cheeses, the demand for which across Australia far out-strips supply. The property is at Gidgegannup, high on a ridge overlooking the Avon Valley, and the Avon River. Rocky and high, it is almost impossible to farm with traditional crops or stock. Goats, organically farmed, fit the bill. Gabrielle and Alan travelled to France to learn traditional techniques of goat rearing and cheese-making. They make frais (fresh cheese), some ash-covered to protect the cheese and to draw out the acidity, as well as a beautifully textured aged cheese that has developed a natural rind.

Dandaragan is not exactly next door, but in country Australia it's not unusual to travel more than an hour or two to do the shopping, or just to drop in for afternoon tea. The farmhouse was built by convicts more than 150 years ago, and the approach to farming was traditional for over 100 of those years. So the decision to go organic was not taken lightly. It means no chemicals for the land or the herd. All the meat is grown in the healthiest way possible, maximising food taste, integrity, and pure goodness.

That evening back at New Norcia we prepared dinner in the monastery's baker's oven for the new friends we had met. We served our guests on the upstairs balcony of the Spanish-inspired New Norcia Hotel. With hundreds of galahs and parrots chiming in for the sunset chorus, we joined our guests for a memorable meal in a memorable setting as the retreating sun painted the horizon pink and orange.

The thing I found fascinating about the people I had met in this region is that all of them, no matter what they produced, seemed to be salt-of-the-earth types. They all have a refreshingly simple respect for the environment and their animals, and a real care and concern for the raw produce that ended up as a brilliant ingredients in our kitchen.

Farinata

For me these are the ultimate nibbly bits — a cool drink, and a plate full of these crispy chickpea crêpes with a simple flavouring just can't be beaten. They also make a great addition to an antipasto platter, or can be eaten just as a snack. The success of this recipe depends on the temperature of the oven and the pan — the hotter the better!

SERVES 4–6

3 cups	besan flour*	750ml
4 cups	water	1 L
	Salt	
1/2 cup	olive oil (approx)	125 mL

Topping

8–10	green crayfish or shrimp, peeled, deveined and sliced	8–10
1 tbsp	fresh rosemary leaves, coarsely chopped	15 mL
	Freshly ground black pepper	

1. Sift the flour into a medium bowl. Gradually stir in the water and mix to a very thin, lump-free batter. Set aside to rest for 30 minutes.

2. Preheat the oven to 500°F (260°C). Place a non-stick or cast-iron skillet with a heatproof handle in the oven to heat to the same temperature. Season the batter with salt, and stir in 1 tbsp (15 mL) oil. Mix well. Carefully remove the skillet from the oven and add enough olive oil to just cover the bottom. Pour in just enough batter to cover the pan in a thin layer. Scatter some crayfish or shrimp pieces on top, and sprinkle with a little rosemary and black pepper.

3. Place in the oven and cook for 8–10 minutes, or until the edges are brown, the centre cooked, and the bottom crisp. Transfer to a wire rack and repeat with the remaining ingredients.

4. Serve hot — it does not matter if it breaks up!

besan flour is also known as gram flour. Besan is available from Indian or Asian markets

Focaccia

The addition of beer stimulates the yeast and adds flavour to the bread. If not needed immediately, one portion of the dough may be wrapped in plastic wrap and frozen for future use.

MAKES TWO 11- X 15-INCH (28- X 38-CM) FOCACCIA

4 cups	semolina flour plus extra	1L
2¹/₂ cups	tepid water	625 mL
1 oz	fresh yeast (or 1/2 oz [15 g] dried yeast*)	30 g
3¹/₂ fl oz	pilsner beer	100 mL
4 cups	bread flour**	1L
1 tbsp	salt	15 mL
¹/₂ cup	olive oil	125 mL
	Coarse sea salt and freshly ground black pepper	

Toppings

· Slow roast unpeeled garlic cloves and fresh rosemary leaves in olive oil, then squeeze out the garlic flesh, and mix with the rosemary and oil.

· Cut vine-ripened tomatoes in half, and season with chopped garlic, thyme, and olive oil.

· Slice fennel very finely, and mix with lemon thyme and olive oil.

* If using dried yeast, mix with ¹/₃ cup (75 mL) of the warm water in a small bowl and leave to activate, 5–8 minutes. If it does not foam, discard and start again with new yeast. Add to the semolina mixture before adding the beer.

** Available from health food stores. Flour packaged as bread flour, hard flour or durum wheat flour is suitable. Do not use bread mix, which is a mix designed for use in bread machines.

① Place the semolina in a large bowl. Gradually add the water, mixing with a wooden spoon to a porridge consistency. Break up the fresh yeast, and mix in by hand. When completely blended, add the beer. When the mixture starts to activate, add the bread flour and salt. Mix with a wooden spoon initially, then use your hands to form a loose dough. Turn out onto a floured surface and knead until springy and smooth, 8–10 minutes. Rest for 5 minutes.

② Divide the dough in half. Dust two baking sheets liberally with semolina flour. Roll each portion out to a flat oval shape about 1-inch (2.5-cm) thick, and transfer to a prepared tray. Using the tips of your fingers, push holes into the surface. If using a topping such as caramelized garlic or herbs, pat it onto the surface now. Cover with a clean, dry tea towel and allow to prove in a warm, breeze-free spot until almost doubled in size, 1¹/₂–2 hours.

③ Preheat the oven to 375°F (190°C). Just before baking, drizzle the oil over each focaccia, and sprinkle with the salt and a little pepper. Transfer to the oven and bake until cooked and golden, 20–25 minutes. Immediately transfer to wire racks to cool.

Smoked beef carpaccio with Mediterranean vegetables and goat cheese

Beef carpaccio is a lovely light way to start a meal. I have smoked the beef in this recipe, which is a different way of incorporating flavour into the meat.

SERVES 6

1¼ lb	centre-cut beef filet	625 g

Curing mixture

10	black peppercorns	10
2 tbsp	sea salt	30 mL
2 tsp	mixed dried herbs, such as sage, thyme, basil, oregano	10 mL
10	juniper berries	10
1 tbsp	paprika	15 mL
5 oz	hickory shavings*	150 g
3½ oz	dried mushrooms (optional)	100 g

Mediterranean vegetables

1	red bell pepper	1
1	green bell pepper	1
1	yellow bell pepper	1
2 tsp	extra-virgin olive oil	10 mL
1	zucchini, sliced	1
1	eggplant, weighing about 8 oz (250 g), cut into ½-inch (1-cm) slices	1
	Salt and freshly ground black pepper	
4	semi-dried tomatoes, sliced into strips	4

* Available from barbecue suppliers.

1. Truss the fillet with kitchen twine at 1-inch (2.5-cm) intervals.

2. To make the curing mixture, place all the ingredients in a mortar and pestle, and crush to a powder. This step can also be done in a spice mill. Rub all over the beef, cover loosely with plastic wrap, and refrigerate for 8–10 hours.

3. Place the hickory shavings in the bottom of a wok and heat over moderately high heat. Once they start to smoke, add the mushrooms. Position a wire rack or steamer in the wok, place the beef on this, and cover with a tight-fitting lid. Reduce the heat to low, and smoke for 5 minutes. Do not lift the lid. Remove from the heat, and rest for 15 minutes to allow the smoke to infuse. Remove the beef and cool.

4. Preheat the grill to hot. Grill the peppers until charred all over. Place in a plastic bag and set aside to cool. Peel off the skin, then cut into slices and dress with half the oil. Grill the zucchini and eggplant, and dress with the remaining oil. Season with salt and pepper.

continued over...

Curtis Stone

Smoked beef carpaccio with Mediterranean vegetables and goats cheese, continued...

Dressing

2³/₄ oz	soft goat cheese, crumbled	75 g
¹/₄ cup	tarragon vinegar	50 mL
2 tbsp	extra-virgin olive oil	30 mL
2 tbsp	peanut oil	30 mL
	Salt and freshly ground black pepper	
1 cup	loosely packed wild arugula	250 mL
	Extra goat cheese for garnish	

5 Using a sharp knife, slice the beef as thinly as possible. Fan the slices, overlapping slightly, on a serving plate. Combine the peppers, zucchini, eggplant and semi-dried tomatoes in a bowl, toss gently, and place in the centre of the beef.

6 To make the dressing, blend the cheese with the vinegar until smooth. Whisk in the extra-virgin olive oil and peanut oil, and season lightly with salt and pepper. Pour enough over the wild arugula to coat lightly, and place this on top of the vegetables. Drizzle the remaining dressing and crumble a little extra goat cheese over the beef just before serving.

Curtis Stone

Confit tomato tartare with green beans and olives

Confit tomatoes have a lovely intense flavour, which is broken up well by the crunchy green beans.

SERVES 4

6	plum tomatoes	6
1 tbsp	olive oil	15 mL
3¹/₂ oz	baby green beans	100 g
2	cloves garlic, thinly sliced	2
¹/₃ cup	extra-virgin olive oil	75 mL
1 tbsp	fresh thyme leaves	15 mL
1	shallot	1
1 tbsp	finely chopped fresh flat-leaf parsley	15 mL
2 tsp	baby capers	10 mL
	Salt and freshly ground black pepper	
3	black Spanish olives, pitted	3
1 tbsp	finely chopped fresh chives	15 mL

1 Preheat the oven to 175°F (80°C). Line a baking sheet with foil. Bring a large saucepan of water to the boil. Core the tomatoes, cut a cross on the opposite end, and plunge into the boiling water for 8–10 seconds. Remove, and refresh in ice water, then peel. Add the olive oil to the saucepan, and blanch the beans until just tender, 1–2 minutes. Drain, and rinse under very cold water to arrest the cooking. Reserve.

2 Quarter the tomatoes lengthways and remove the seeds, leaving petal-shaped pieces of flesh. Spread over the prepared baking sheet, and place a slice of garlic on each one. Drizzle with 2¹/₂ tbsp (45 mL) extra-virgin olive oil, and sprinkle the thyme over the top. Place in the oven for 1¹/₂ hours. Cool, then dice, and place in a bowl.

3 Cut the shallot to the same size as the tomatoes, and add to the bowl. Add the parsley and capers, and season with salt and pepper. Toss lightly. Place the top (the ring-shaped wall) of a 7-inch (1.5 L) springform pan in the centre of a serving plate, and fill with the tomato tartare. Gently lift the ring off to leave a circular mound of tomato tartare.

4 Slice the olives in half lengthways, and place around the tartare. Trim the beans, and arrange on top of the tartare in a lattice pattern. Mix the chives with the remaining extra-virgin olive oil. Drizzle around the plate and serve.

Curtis Stone

Butternut squash and goat cheese caponata

I read somewhere that caponata in ancient Latin recipes usually involved seafood, but it slowly evolved to using vegetables as economic pressures forced frugality. Caponata generally relies on the balance of a sweet taste with sharp or sour flavours, and this recipe is a perfect combination of the two.

SERVES 4

1¹/₄ lb	butternut squash, peeled	625 g
2	cloves garlic, thinly sliced	2
2	dried red chilies, crumbled	2
1	cinnamon stick, broken into slivers	1
2 tbsp	fresh sage leaves	30 mL
7 fl oz	olive oil	200 mL
¹/₃ cup	balsamic vinegar	75 mL
	Salt and freshly ground black pepper	
3 tbsp	sugar	45 mL
2 cups	loosely packed wild arugula	500 mL
¹/₂	lemon, quartered	¹/₂
2 oz	goat cheese, crumbled	60 g

1 Preheat the oven to 325°F (160°C), and line a baking sheet with waxed paper. Cut the squash into 1-inch (2.5-cm) slices. Halve these diagonally to give half-moon shapes. Place in a large bowl with the garlic, chilies, cinnamon and sage. Add 1 tbsp (15 mL) oil and 2 tbsp (30 mL) vinegar, and season with salt and pepper. Toss to distribute evenly, then leave for 10 minutes.

2 Spread the squash in a single layer on the prepared baking sheet, and bake in the oven until soft and the edges crispy, about 30 minutes. If some is burnt just pick it out.

3 Meanwhile, place the sugar in a small saucepan, and melt over a low heat. Continue cooking until it changes to a light gold colour. Remove from the heat, and gradually stir in the remaining vinegar. Return to the heat, and stir until smooth. Allow to cool.

4 Stir the remaining oil into the sugar and vinegar mixture to make a dressing. Toss half with the squash to coat well, then transfer to a large serving plate. Toss the remaining dressing with the arugula. Add a squeeze of lemon. Scatter the goat cheese over the squash, and garnish with the dressed arugula, and the lemon wedges.

Wild mushroom risotto

As far as risotto goes my opinion is that anyone who doesn't like it has never eaten one that has been made correctly. If you can get your hands on porcini mushrooms, they are brilliant. The technique used here can be adapted to any kind of risotto you like and because it is an easy thing to cook for a large volume of people, it is a winner for a dinner party.

SERVES 4

3 cups	chicken stock	750 mL
6 tbsp	butter	90 mL
1 lb	fresh wild mushrooms (such as pine, portobello or porcini), sliced	500 g
4	shallots, chopped	4
4	cloves garlic, finely chopped	4
1 tbsp	chopped fresh thyme leaves	15 mL
2/3 lb	arborio rice	350 g
7 fl oz	dry white wine	200 mL
3 1/2 oz	aged pecorino cheese, finely grated	100 g
1 tbsp	chopped fresh flat-leaf parsley	15 mL
	Salt and freshly ground black pepper	
	Shaved aged pecorino cheese to garnish	

1. Pour the stock into a saucepan, and bring to the boil. Reduce the heat, and maintain at a low simmer. Preheat a deep skillet over medium heat, and add 1 tbsp (15 mL) butter. Add the mushrooms and fry quickly until golden. Remove and reserve. Add half the remaining butter to the pan, and lightly fry the shallots, garlic and thyme until softened, but not coloured, 1–2 minutes. Add the rice, and stir for 1 minute to coat the grains.

2. Add the wine, increase the heat slightly, and cook, stirring often, until it has almost completely evaporated. Stir in a ladleful of the hot stock, then reduce the heat to medium. Cook, stirring often, until the stock has been absorbed. Add another ladleful of stock, and continue in this way for 10 minutes, then stir through the reserved mushrooms. Continue adding stock until it is all used and the rice is al dente, 8–10 minutes. If the stock runs out before the rice is ready, use hot water. The consistency should be moist but not mushy.

3. Remove from the heat, and add the remaining butter, the grated pecorino and the parsley. Season to taste with salt and pepper, and stir until the butter melts. Serve, garnished with the pecorino shavings.

Curtis Stone

Vitello tonnato

This is a classic Italian starter usually found in the north. The combination of veal and tuna is delightful. You will need a long sharp knife, as it can be a bit tricky to slice poached meat. The dressing is like a tuna mayonnaise, and also works well in salads.

SERVES 4–6

2 lb	veal fillet, trimmed of fat	1 kg

Dressing

2	free-range egg yolks	2
	Juice of 3 lemons	
15	capers	15
1	shallot, finely chopped	1
7 oz	canned tuna in oil, drained	200 g
7 fl oz	peanut oil	200 mL
7 fl oz	olive oil (approx)	200 mL
	Salt and freshly ground black pepper	

Extra capers to garnish

Caper berries to garnish

1. Put a large saucepan of water on to boil. Reduce the heat to a point just below simmering, 150°F (65°C). Using a large sheet of plastic wrap, tightly roll up the veal, covering it completely so that it resembles a sausage. Twist and knot both ends to seal. Place in the hot water and poach for 1 hour. Check the heat from time to time, and maintain it at just below simmering. Remove from the pot, plunge into ice water to stop the cooking process.

2. To make the dressing, place the egg yolks in a food processor and blend. Add the lemon juice, capers and shallot, and process for 1 minute. Add the tuna, and process for a further 2 minutes. With the motor still running, gradually add the peanut oil in a steady trickle. Slowly drizzle in the olive oil, tasting as you go (the flavour of the olive oil may become a little too powerful). If the dressing becomes too thick, add a little hot water. Pass through a fine sieve, and season to taste with salt and pepper.

3. To serve, spread a circle of dressing over the centre of a serving platter. Remove the veal from the plastic wrap and slice thinly. Arrange the slices in a fan over the dressing and garnish with capers and caper berries.

Curtis Stone

Roast leg of lamb wrapped in rosemary

There is really nothing like the flavour of this dish: the way the rosemary penetrates the meat with its flavour, and the resulting pan juices are awesome. Don't skimp on the rosemary. A top tip to check that roasted lamb is cooked, is to take a knife, and make an incision like a pocket in the length of the leg bone towards the shank. Place 1 or 2 fingers in the incision and if the meat feels warm to hot it is cooked.

SERVES 4–6

4 lb	leg of lamb, hip joint removed (sometimes sold as Ezicarve)	2 kg
4	cloves garlic, cut into slivers	4
6	anchovy fillets, quartered	6
	Freshly ground black pepper	
2 tbsp	olive oil	30 mL
10–12	large sprigs fresh rosemary	10–12
3¹/₂ oz	black olive paste*	100 g
1 tbsp	freshly squeezed lemon juice	15 mL

1 Hang or rest the lamb in a cool, dry spot until it is dry to the touch. This makes all the difference to the flavour. Trim off and discard any excess fat. Make incisions all over the meat using a small sharp knife, creating small pockets about knuckle deep. Stuff a garlic sliver and a piece of anchovy into each incision, then season the surface well with pepper.

2 Heat half the oil in a flameproof heavy-duty roasting pan, and brown the lamb on all sides over a moderately high heat. Allow to cool.

3 Preheat the oven to 400°F (200°C). Stretch a good length of kitchen string along the work surface, and overlap the sprigs of rosemary along the length of the string. Smear the lamb with the olive paste, and place it on the rosemary at one end. Roll it up so that it's completely encased in the rosemary and tie the string tightly to secure. It doesn't matter how crudely you do this — as long as the rosemary stays in place.

continued over...

4 Return the lamb to the roasting pan, drizzle with the remaining oil and the lemon juice and place in the oven. Roast for 15 minutes per 1 lb (500 g), plus 15 minutes more, turning occasionally to cook evenly. Remove from the oven and rest the meat for one-third of the time it took to cook. This ensures a perfectly pink result. Reserve the rosemary for garnish, carve and serve.

* Where black olive paste is unavailable, use 3¹/₂ oz (100 g) pitted kalamata olives and purée.

Ben O'Donoghue

Fresh fig, honey, and rosemary calzone

This is one of those odd Italian combinations that was shown to me by an Italian chef friend in London. He used grapes, but this combination works just as well.

MAKES 8 INDIVIDUAL CALZONE

1/2	batch Focaccia dough (see page 121)	
6	ripe figs, stalks removed	6
1/3 cup	mascarpone cheese	75 mL
1/3 cup	olive oil	75 mL
2 tbsp	honey	30 mL
2 tsp	chopped fresh rosemary leaves	10 mL
	Extra olive oil for brushing	
8	sprigs fresh rosemary	
	Icing sugar for dusting	
	Ground cinnamon for dusting	

1. Place the dough in an oiled bowl and cover with plastic wrap. Leave in a warm spot until almost doubled in size, about 1 1/2 hours.

2. Preheat the oven to 400°F (200°C), and line two baking sheets with waxed paper. Knock the dough down and divide into 8 equal balls. Roll out on a well-floured work surface to form a 3–4 inch (8–10-cm) disc 1/8-inch (3-mm) thick.

3. Slice the figs into 4 wedges. Place the wedges side by side along the centre of each disc of dough. Add about 1 tsp (5 mL) mascarpone and 1 tsp (5 mL) olive oil, then drizzle with a little honey and sprinkle some rosemary over the top. Brush the rims of the discs with additional oil. Fold half of the dough over the top of the figs to encase them, forming a half-moon shape. Press the rims of dough together to seal, and crimp the edges with a fork.

4. Place on the prepared baking sheets, ensuring they are well spaced. Brush with more oil, drizzle with a little extra honey and place a sprig of rosemary on top. Bake for 15–20 minutes, until crisp and golden. Immediately transfer to wire racks to cool. Serve warm, dusted with icing sugar and a sprinkling of cinnamon. Delicious with vanilla ice cream.

Orange granita with mascarpone

I always say that you should eat for the season and climate. On a hot summer's day you need something refreshing, so a granita is perfect. You can make granita from almost anything — from fruit juices to Champagne. They are a great palate cleanser, so may be served between courses.

SERVES 4

3 cups	water	750 mL
10 oz	instant dissolving sugar	300 g
	Finely grated rind of 2 small oranges	
1 cup	freshly squeezed orange juice, chilled	250 mL
1/4 cup	freshly squeezed lemon juice	50 mL
	Extra 3 oranges	3
1/3 cup	Muscat or dessert wine	75 mL
1 cup	mascarpone cheese, softened	250 mL

1 Place 2 cups (500 mL) water in a saucepan with 1/4 cup (50 mL) sugar. Add the rind, and bring slowly to the boil. Remove from the heat, and strain into a bowl. Stir in the orange and lemon juice, and place in the freezer. Once ice crystals start to form — in about 15–20 minutes — stir the mixture with a fork to break them up. Return to the freezer, and continue this procedure until the mixture resembles snow.

2 To make the confit orange rind, using a sharp knife or a vegetable peeler, thinly peel the 3 oranges, ensuring that no pith is left on the peel. Slice it into thin strips. Place in a saucepan, cover with cold water, and bring to the boil. Strain, then return to the empty saucepan, and add remaining water and sugar. Slowly bring to the boil, reduce heat to very low, and simmer for 1 1/2–2 hours.

3 Mix the Muscat into the mascarpone, and place in the bottom of 4 dessert glasses. Place a large spoonful of granita on top, and garnish with the confit orange rind.

Curtis Stone

Tasmania

Tasmania

Strahan, Wild Salmon, and Gruff

Ben O'Donoghue

Tasmania has a rich and unique history, and where once its economy was based on mining, agriculture and primary resources, today eco-tourism and the production of gourmet food products are the key ingredients to Tasmania's success.

The thing I noticed about Tasmania the first time I went there was the weather. It's milder than the mainland, and the island climate ensures that the varied localized weather systems keep the island green and clean. Every time I've been, it's been sunny and beautiful. Interestingly, Hobart is statistically the second driest city in Australia, yet close by there is an abundance of temperate rainforest, mountainscapes where snow falls, and thick dense forests. Hobart is also the second oldest Australian capital city. Settlers and convicts first came to what was then called Van Diemen's Land in 1803. Convicts continued to be transported there from England, often for petty crimes, until 1853. They played a major part in the colony's early development providing labour and skills, such as building and architecture. The convicts and their warders added a dark side to the history of the island, with foreboding places like Port Arthur, and the entrance to Macquarie Harbour in Strahan known as 'Hell's Gates'. A prison sentence in Tasmania struck fear into many hearts.

Strahan, where we spent most of our time, is located in a natural amphitheatre overlooking the vast, protected Macquarie Harbour, a safe anchorage on the notorious and rugged west coast. There's nothing to stop the waves of the Roaring Forties between here and South Africa. Macquarie Harbour is almost 80 square nautical miles, which is almost six times the size of Sydney Harbour.

There's an amusing story of a group of convicts in Strahan who, after building a sailing ship under the watchful eyes of their guards, stole the ship in the middle of the night, and sailed it

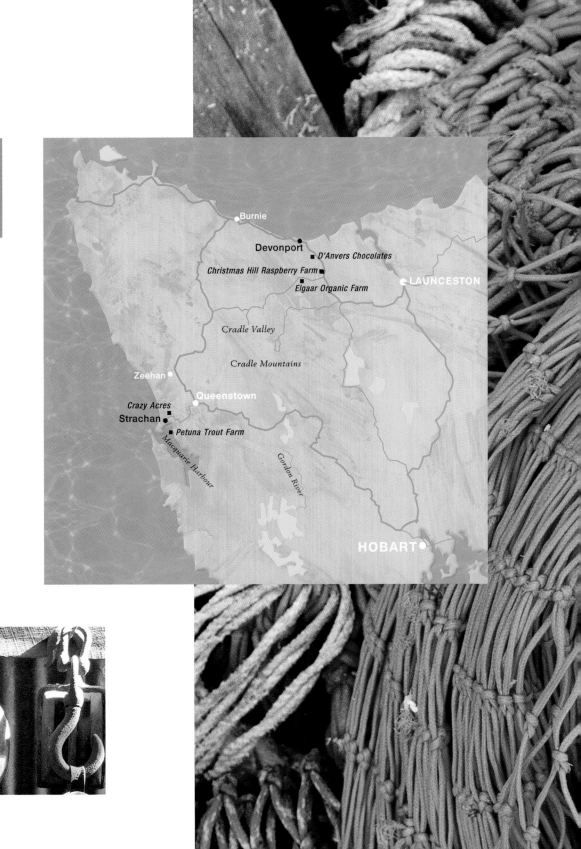

Burnie

Devonport
D'Anvers Chocolates
Christmas Hill Raspberry Farm
Elgaar Organic Farm

LAUNCESTON

Cradle Valley

Cradle Mountains

Zeehan

Queenstown

Crazy Acres
Strachan
Petuna Trout Farm

Macquarie Harbour

Gordon River

HOBART

to South America. Remarkably they made it, but were recaptured, and extradited to England to stand trial. At the trial it came to light that because the ship had yet to be commissioned it could not therefore be classed as a ship, so the convicts had their charges altered to 'stealing lumber'. Their punishment was to be transported back to Strahan to, I presume, build more ships. I find it amazing that Prisoners of Her Majesty (POHMs) were sent to a place like Strahan, which to me looks more like paradise than hell — it is picture postcard stuff.

Many tourists flock to Strahan to experience its unhurried pace, and to experience the magnificent World Heritage Area of the Gordon River, and the ancient Huon pine forests.

Tasmania's building heritage is well preserved, and the landscape is dotted with European-inspired sandstone and brick buildings in abundance. With the predominant colour being green, these buildings give the international visitor the impression that they haven't left Europe at all. Driving through some towns felt just like being in Devon or Wales.

Apart from the history there were two other reasons to include Tasmania on our itinerary. First, since we'd been away, this tiny island had been developing an incredible reputation for first-class food and agricultural produce. Whereas once Tassie evoked images of apples, and more bloody apples, today it's Pinot Noir, smoked salmon, lobsters, ocean trout, wild berries, truffles, matured cheeses, Brie, and much more. The second reason was to meet up with a long-time mate of mine Steve (whom we call Herb, so we don't get him mixed up with his dad), and Herb's dad (also Steve, obviously), whom everyone calls Gruff. Gruff lives on a 20-acre (8-hectare) property called Crazy Acres, just outside Strahan. Gruff loves a drink, listening to a yarn, AC/DC and C & W, and fishing. He's a kind of Aussie Osborne, a real character, and so are all his mates.

Let's start at the beginning of this journey. We drove the jeep onto the trans-Tasman ferry in Melbourne, wandered upstairs to put our gear into the cabin, then settled down at the bar to have a drink or two, and a chat with some fellow travellers. The new car ferry is quite popular. After leaving port

at around nine in the evening, we arrived in Devonport at six in the morning, feeling refreshed after a good night's sleep. Herb was waiting for us in Strahan, and, so as not to arrive empty-handed, we headed out to search for some local delicacies.

A short drive along the highway from Devonport we called in at D'Anvers chocolates. (D'Anvers means 'from Antwerp', I'm told.) Curtis and I believe that anytime is the right time for good chocolate, and so we headed in. There we met Igor Van Gerwen, a Belgium-born and trained chocolatier who now calls Tasmania home. He invited us into his kitchen — there is nothing better than the smell of warm chocolate. D'Anvers makes everything by hand and so their maximum output is just about 2200 pounds (1000 kilograms) per week.

Some of Igor's staff were piping traditional truffles, then coating them in dark chocolate, and rolling them in shaved almonds. They let us have a go ourselves. Luckily part of a chef's training is piping all sorts of things, so we soon got the hang of it. The chocolate also inspired Curtis, and he took some white couverture chocolate with him.

The basic difference between couverture chocolate (the kind Igor uses), and compound chocolate (the kind you buy in block form) is twofold. The first is that couverture chocolate is made with a relatively expensive ingredient, cocoa butter. Compound chocolate uses animal fat or vegetable margarine instead. That's what can leave the slightly greasy texture in the mouth. The second difference is that compound chocolate has a fineness of 30 to 35 microns, while Igor's couverture chocolate is 10 to 12 microns. In other words, it's three times finer. This means it's smoother on the palate, and simply melts away on the tongue, leaving just a rich chocolate taste to savour.

Just a little further on we saw a roadside sign for fresh raspberries, and stopped in at the Christmas Hill Raspberry Farm. Lindi Dourauf took us down past the lake to where the raspberries grow in rows on the hillside. Lindi has twelve different varieties planted over 10 acres (4 hectares), which are all picked by hand. The raspberries are available fresh from late summer through autumn, and snap frozen the rest of the year. I couldn't pick the subtle differences between the varieties, even with careful sampling during the Ben-style picking: one for me, one for the bucket …

We next tracked down Joe and Antonia Gretschmann at Elgaar Organic Farm. Although the Gretschmanns have been in Australia for two decades, their family has been making cheeses in Germany since the 1450s. Their farm is completely organic, and built according to time-honoured plans. The cellars, for example, are built of stone, and are completely underground in the Bavarian style. The temperature in there is cool, even slightly cold, which is achieved without any air-conditioning or cooling. I was impressed by how simply things worked: where the sun hits the building, the cellar is dry; on the other side, the cellar is moist.

The cheeses are part-made in an impressive Swiss copper vat that shines brightly as the result of liberally applied elbow grease. As in Europe, the cellars have their own natural flora and no foreign starter cultures need to be introduced. The Gretschmanns make their own starter culture in a method that has been handed down for generations. This fascinated us but despite numerous attempts, we were unable to get even a hint of how it is done. Many Elgaar cheeses are supplied to restaurants on the mainland. They are stored at the farm until they are needed, and on request are freighted one by one. And it is not just fabulous cheeses that the Gretschmanns produce. They also produce milk (in bottles, no less), yoghurt, mascarpone, and cultured, unsalted butter in a traditional wooden German churn.

Our next stop was to Petuna Seafoods ocean trout farm located in the perfectly pristine Macquarie Harbour, a short boat-ride from Strahan, and on the edge of the World Heritage Wilderness Area. The scenery is breathtaking. Strahan harbour is perfect for farming ocean trout because the fish require both fresh and salt water to thrive. In this unique place, fresh water flows in a top layer from the famous Franklin and Gordon rivers, while salt water from the Southern Ocean flows a little deeper through the massive pens. Another reason this environment is so perfect is that the naturally stained waters of the harbour protect the fish from sunburn!

The trout are reared from the beginning in hatcheries in the north of Tasmania, and then, after about twelve months, they are transferred to the pens in Macquarie Harbour. The fish grow to about 4–8 pounds (2–4 kilograms) before they are harvested. Each pen holds approximately 7000 fish, and over 3000 pounds (1500 tonnes) of ocean trout and Atlantic salmon are harvested each year. That's a heck of a lot of sushi!

When we eventually made it to Strahan, through some of the most beautiful countryside in the world, what we really needed was a cleansing ale with Herb and Gruff. The boys didn't let us down. Strahan was once a sleepy little spot on the map, but today it's a vibrant village with tourists and locals flocking to mix in the local café and waterfront pub. I have always loved coming to Tassie. It's a big-hearted place full of real people in a genuinely beautiful part of the world. No wonder I keep coming back.

Red-skinned potato, olive, and caper salad

I love these waxy potatoes. They're so full of flavour, and they make the best potato salad you will come across. If you can't get them use a fingerling potato, which has a similarly pleasant flavour and texture.

SERVES 4–6

2 lb	red-skinned potatoes, unpeeled	1 kg
1/2	clove garlic	1/2
	Salt	
2 tbsp	coarsely chopped flat-leaf parsley	30 mL
3 1/2 oz	baby capers (if salted, soak in cold water for 30 minutes and rinse well)	100 g
7 oz	large green olives, pitted	200 g
2 tbsp	white wine vinegar	30 mL
3 1/2 fl oz	extra-virgin olive oil	100 mL
	Freshly ground black pepper	
	Finely grated rind of 1 lemon	
2 tbsp	white celery leaves	30 mL

1 Place the potatoes in a large saucepan and cover with cold water. Add salt, bring to the boil and simmer for about 20 minutes, depending on size, until tender. In a large mortar, smash the garlic with a little salt, then add half the parsley and roughly smash. Add the capers and olives and do the same to give a coarse, roughly broken up texture.

2 Drain, peel and cut the potatoes in half while still hot. Add the vinegar and oil. Cool for 10 minutes, then add the olive and parsley mixture. Season with salt and pepper, and toss through the rind, celery leaves and remaining parsley.

3 Great served with fish or poached chicken.

Ben O'Donoghue

Smoked salmon with fennel and dillweed salad

I find when you are serving seafood it is very nice to break up the texture with something crisp or crunchy. The fennel and dillweed salad is actually like a pickle so it remains very crunchy and fresh, which cuts through the richness of the salmon.

SERVES 4

2	baby fennel bulbs, trimmed	2
3¹/₂ oz	coarse rock salt	100 g
1¹/₄ cups	water	300 mL
7 oz	instant dissolving sugar	200 g
¹/₃ cup	white wine vinegar	75 mL
¹/₂ cup	finely chopped dillweed	125 mL
¹/₃ cup	extra-virgin olive oil	75 mL
1 tbsp	lemon juice	15 mL
	Salt and freshly ground black pepper	
7 oz	sliced smoked salmon	200 g

❶ Slice the fennel on a mandoline or use the thinnest blade on a food processor to give slices that are almost transparent. Place in a bowl and toss with the salt. Set aside for 10 minutes. Place the water, sugar and vinegar in a saucepan and bring to just below boiling point. Remove from the heat. Wash the salt from the fennel under running water. Place the fennel in a clean bowl and pour the vinegar mixture over the top. Cover and set aside for 12 hours.

❷ Mix half the dillweed with the fennel. Combine the remaining dillweed with the oil, and lemon juice. Season with salt and pepper. Arrange the smoked salmon around the edge of a serving platter. Squeeze the excess liquid from the fennel, and pile the fennel in the centre of the platter. Sprinkle with more pepper and drizzle the dillweed dressing around the outside of the platter.

Curtis Stone

Stuffed zucchini-flower fritters with wild arugula pesto

Anyone who has ever had a vegetable garden will know that on the end of a zucchini grows a small flower. These flowers have a taste similar to the zucchini but a little milder. The nature of the flower enables us to stuff them with all sorts of flavoursome ingredients.

If your local greengrocer doesn't stock them ask for some to be ordered for you, once you start to demand them, they will supply them.

SERVES 4

5 oz	ricotta cheese	150 g
1/2 tsp	freshly squeezed lemon juice	2 mL
4	fresh basil leaves, shredded	4
2 oz	Parmesan cheese, freshly grated	60 g
	Salt and freshly ground black pepper	
12	zucchini flowers	12

Batter

3/4 cup	all-purpose flour	175 mL
1/2 cup	soda water	125 mL
	Vegetable oil for deep-frying	
	Seasoned all-purpose flour for dusting	
1/2 cup	loosely packed fresh basil leaves	125 mL
	Extra freshly grated Parmesan cheese for serving	

1 Mix the ricotta, lemon juice, basil and Parmesan in a bowl, and season with salt and pepper. Cut the stalks off the zucchini flowers, leaving 1/2 inch (1 cm) attached. Slice the stalks in half lengthways. Open a flower and, depending on its size, spoon 1–2 tsp (5–10 mL) cheese mixture into the cavity until two-thirds full. Twist the end of the petals to close up. Repeat with the remaining cheese mixture and flowers.

2 To make the batter, mix the flour and soda water with a spoon until smooth.

3 Fill a large saucepan with vegetable oil to a depth of 4 inches (10 cm) and heat. When hot, dust the stuffed flowers and stalks with the seasoned flower. Dip into the batter and fry in batches until golden brown. Remove from the oil and place on paper towels to drain. Deep-fry the basil leaves in the hot oil and drain on paper towels.

continued over...

Curtis Stone

4 Sprinkle the flowers and stalks with the Parmesan and serve at once, topped with the fried basil leaves, and accompanied by wild arugula pesto.

Wild arugula pesto

3^1/$_2$ oz	*toasted pine nuts*	*100 g*
3 oz	*freshly grated Parmesan cheese*	*90 g*
1	*clove garlic, minced*	*1*
1 cup	*loosely packed wild arugula leaves*	*250 mL*
1 cup	*loosely packed flat-leaf parsley*	*250 mL*
1 tsp	*freshly squeezed lemon juice*	*5 mL*
^{1}/$_4$ cup	*extra-virgin olive oil*	*50 mL*
	Salt and freshly ground black pepper	

1 Place the pine nuts, Parmesan, garlic, arugula and parsley in a food processor, and pulse until finely chopped. Add the lemon juice and pulse to blend.

2 With the motor running, gradually add the olive oil in a trickle. Season with salt and pepper.

Curtis Stone

Salt-baked onion with truffled egg

In Tasmania's cooler climate the vegetables grow more slowly and therefore have a greater intensity of flavour. The root vegies, especially, benefit from this climate. Having heard that they were growing truffles here I thought the combination of flavours in this recipe would be quite exciting. If fresh truffles prove too expensive, then truffle oil works really well — just don't use too much. This dish is a real winter warmer.

SERVES 4

2 lb	rock salt	1 kg
4	large organic brown onions, unpeeled	4
4	sprigs fresh rosemary	4
2 tsp	butter	10 mL
1	clove garlic, minced	1
1 cup	18% cream	250 mL
3½ oz	Taleggio cheese, cubed	100 g
	Salt and freshly ground black pepper	
4	free-range egg yolks	4
½ tsp	truffle oil	2 mL
2 oz	Parmesan cheese, freshly grated	60 g

❶ Preheat the oven to 300°F (150°C). Spread the salt in the base of a roasting pan. Prick a hole in the top of each onion with a small knife and push in a sprig of rosemary. Place on the salt in the prepared pan, transfer to the oven and roast until soft, about 1 hour.

❷ Remove from the oven and lift the onions off the salt. Allow to cool for 10 minutes. Slice the top quarter off each onion and reserve for a lid. Scoop out and reserve each onion centre, leaving a thin (1–2 layers) outer shell. Roughly mince the reserved onion centre.

❸ Melt the butter in a saucepan, and gently cook the minced onion and garlic until sweet and golden brown, 8–10 minutes. Add the cream, and reduce by half. Remove from the heat, and add the Taleggio. Stir until melted, and season to taste with salt and pepper. Return the onion shells to the salted pan and half fill with the creamed onion. Gently place an egg yolk on top, and sprinkle each with 2–3 drops of oil. Top with the remaining creamed onion mixture. Sprinkle with the Parmesan cheese, return to the oven and bake until golden, about 10 minutes. Serve with a salad of bitter salad leaves dressed with balsamic vinegar.

Ben O'Donoghue

Rock oysters Florentine

Oysters cook very quickly, so need only a little time under the grill. The lovely velvety consistency of the hollandaise sauce makes this a luxurious dish.

SERVES 4

24	rock oysters (any oysters will do), freshly opened	24
3 lb	rock salt	1.5 kg
2 tsp	butter	10 mL
7 oz	baby spinach leaves	200 g
	Salt and freshly ground black pepper	
2/3 cup	hollandaise sauce*	150 mL
24	sprigs fresh chervil to garnish	24

1 Remove the oysters from their shells and place in a saucepan with their juices. Clean and dry the shells. Spread the rock salt over a roasting pan, and place the oyster shells on top.

2 Melt the butter in a saucepan, add the spinach and fry until just wilted. Transfer to a clean tea towel, and squeeze out excess moisture. Season lightly with salt and pepper. Place a small amount in each oyster shell.

3 Preheat the grill to hot. Warm the oysters and their juices quickly over a moderate heat. Return to their shells, on top of the spinach. Spoon $1^1/_2$ tsp (7 mL) hollandaise sauce over each oyster. Place the roasting pan under the grill and cook until the sauce on the oysters is hot and golden. Garnish with the chervil and serve at once.

*See page 47 and make the Béarnaise sauce, leaving out the tarragon leaves.

Curtis Stone

Warm salad of grilled smoked eel

I absolutely love smoked eel, its rich oiliness is fantastic set against the sharp crispiness of this salad. It's a fantastic, light way to start a meal. If these devilish little creatures aren't your cup of tea then use smoked trout or smoked salmon; just don't grill the stuff. Serve them cold as their textures are less firm and not suitable for grilling.

SERVES 4

1	large fennel bulb	1
1	medium red onion	1
1/2	head radicchio	1/2
1 cup	lightly packed fresh flat-leaf parsley	250 mL
1 cup	loosely packed fresh sorrel leaves	250 mL
10 oz	smoked eel, skinned and boned	300 g
4 tsp	extra-virgin olive oil	20 mL
	Salt and freshly ground black pepper	
1	lemon, halved	1

❶ Trim the fennel, reserving the green tops. Slice thinly across the bulb, and place in ice water to crisp up. Halve the onion lengthways, and slice lengthways. Place in a bowl. Separate the radicchio leaves, and tear into small pieces, discarding the white centre of each leaf. Add the radicchio, parsley, and sorrel to the onion.

❷ Cut the smoked eel into four equal fillets and brush with a little oil. Heat a skillet to high and sear the eel on both sides for 2–3 minutes.

❸ Meanwhile, drain the fennel, and add to the onion and radicchio. Season to taste with salt and pepper, and add the remaining oil and the juice of half the lemon. Break up the reserved fennel tops and add to the salad. Toss gently.

❹ Remove the eel from the pan and squeeze a little lemon over the top. Crumble into the salad and serve.

Salt-baked ocean trout

Fantastic for a summer lunch or dinner.

SERVES 10

2 lb	inexpensive black olives	1 kg
11 lb	rock salt*	5 kg
2	egg whites, lightly whisked	2
4 lb	whole ocean trout (freshly gutted, with the gills removed)**	2 kg
1	bunch fresh rosemary	1
2	lemons, sliced	2

* *It might be less expensive to buy this quantity of rock salt from a hardware shop or pool shop.*
** *If your oven is a standard domestic one, buy two whole ocean trout about 3 lb (1.5 kg) in size, and use two roasting pans. There will be enough salt crust to cover both.*

① To prepare the salt crust, place the olives in a food processor, stones and all, and pulse to chop well. Transfer to a large bowl, then add the salt and egg whites. Mix well.

② In a roasting pan large enough to hold the trout, using half of the salt, make a bed 1-inch (2.5-cm) thick in the shape of the fish. Place the trout on top. Stuff the rosemary and lemon slices into the cavity of the fish to prevent the salt from getting in and making it overly salty.

③ Preheat the oven to 350°F (180°C). Cover the fish with the remaining salt to a thickness similar to the bottom. If need be, use scrunched up foil to make a retaining wall around the outside to hold the salt in place. Place in the oven and bake for 20 minutes. Remove from the oven and check that the fish is cooked by inserting a small knife or roasting fork into the thickest part. Touch it to your lips and if it's warm, the fish is done. Allow to rest for 10 minutes before removing the crust.

④ Using a serrated knife, saw around the base, being careful not to cut into the flesh of the fish. Lift the salt top off; it may come away in one piece or break into several pieces. Brush any excess salt off the fish with a wet pastry brush.

⑤ To serve, peel back the skin, and cut down the centre of the fish, removing the flesh in portions. It should be wonderfully moist and pink.

Veal escalopes with wild mushrooms, mozzarella, and Madeira sauce

Veal is a lovely meat that cooks very quickly. If you overcook veal, it can get quite dry. By serving mozzarella and pasta with the veal escalopes you end up with a lovely moist dish.

SERVES 4

Tomato fondue

6–8	large ripe plum tomatoes	6–8
2 tsp	extra-virgin olive oil	10 mL
1	small shallot, finely chopped	1
1	clove garlic, minced	1
1	fresh bay leaf	1
1	sprig fresh thyme	1
2 tbsp	olive oil	30 mL
1	shallot, finely chopped	1
1	clove garlic, minced	1
7 oz	mixed wild mushrooms (portobello, Swiss brown, chanterelles, pine), sliced	200 g
	Salt and freshly ground black pepper	
3/4 cup	chopped fresh flat-leaf parsley	175 mL
10 oz	fresh tagliatelle	300 g
1 tsp	warm water	5 mL
4	veal escalopes cut from the loin, weighing about 4 oz (125 g) each	4
1	buffalo mozzarella ball, cut into 8 slices	1

1 To make the tomato fondue, core the tomatoes and slice a cross in their tops. Plunge into a saucepan of boiling water for 12–15 seconds. Peel and dice when cool enough to handle. Heat the oil in a saucepan, and add the shallot and garlic. Fry, without colouring, over low heat for 2–3 minutes. Add the tomato, bay leaf, and thyme. Partially cover, and cook, stirring often, over low heat for 2–2$^{1}/_{2}$ hours, until dry and thick. Push through a sieve into a smaller saucepan and keep warm.

2 Heat 2 tsp (10 mL) oil in a medium skillet, and add the shallot and garlic. Fry, without browning, for 1 minute. Increase the heat, and add the mushrooms. Cook, stirring, for 1$^{1}/_{2}$–2 minutes. Season with salt and pepper, and add half the parsley. Keep warm.

3 Meanwhile, bring a large saucepan of water to the boil. Add the tagliatelle and cook until al dente. Drain. Place in a bowl with 2 tsp (10 mL) oil and the water. Season with salt and pepper, and sprinkle with the remaining parsley.

continued over...

Curtis Stone

4 Heat the remaining oil in a large skillet. Season the veal, fry in batches over moderately high heat for 1 minute on each side. Remove from the pan and spread 1 side with a little tomato fondue.

5 Preheat the grill to hot. Arrange 2 slices of mozzarella over the tomato fondue on each escalope. Place under the grill for 10 seconds, until the cheese is soft.

6 To serve, pile a quarter of the tagliatelle in the centre of each of 4 serving plates. Place the veal on top, and arrange the wild mushrooms around the outside. Garnish with the remaining tomato fondue, and drizzle with Madeira sauce.

Madeira sauce

1 tbsp	olive oil	15 mL
3¹/₂ oz	veal trimmings (available from butcher)	100 g
2	shallots, finely sliced	2
2	cloves garlic, minced	2
2 oz	mushrooms, sliced	60 g
1	sprig fresh thyme	1
3	fresh bay leaves	3
5	white peppercorns	5
1 tbsp	sherry vinegar	15 mL
1 tbsp	cognac	15 mL
1¹/₄ cups	Madeira	300 mL
1¹/₄ cups	veal stock	300 mL
¹/₄ cup	water	50 mL

1 Heat the oil in a large skillet, and fry the veal over moderately high heat until golden brown. Add the shallots, garlic, mushrooms, thyme, bay leaves and peppercorns and cook for 5 minutes, stirring often. Add the vinegar, and cook until all the liquid has evaporated. Add the cognac, and stir to deglaze the pan.

2 Pour in the Madeira, and simmer until reduced by two-thirds, 12–15 minutes. Add the stock and water, and bring to the boil. Simmer for 20 minutes, removing any scum that rises to the surface. Pass through a fine sieve into a small saucepan and keep warm.

Curtis Stone

Raspberry and almond tart

Raspberries rock! Here their sharp berry flavour contrasts with the crumbly sweet pastry and the nutty, buttery flavour of the frangipane filling. Serve with 35% whipping cream for a sensual touch to a classic tart. Wicked!

SERVES 8–10

Pastry

10¹/₂ oz	all-purpose flour	320 g
3¹/₂ oz	icing sugar	100 g
8 oz	cold unsalted butter, cubed	250 g
3	free-range egg yolks	3

Filling

8 oz	cold unsalted butter, cubed	250 g
8 oz	instant dissolving sugar	250 g
1	vanilla bean, split in half lengthways	1
8 oz	ground almonds	250 g
Pinch	salt	
1¹/₂ lb	fresh raspberries	750 g
	Icing sugar to serve	

1. To make the pastry, place the flour, sugar and butter in a food processor, and blend to a fine bread crumb texture. Add the egg yolks, 1 at a time, and process until the dough just comes together. Wrap in plastic wrap, and freeze for 30 minutes.

2. To make the filling, combine the butter and sugar in a food processor to give a soft but not overly whipped mixture. Scrape in the vanilla seeds, and add the almond meal and salt. Mix thoroughly.

3. Grease an 11-inch (28-cm) fluted loose-bottomed tart pan. Grate half of the pastry into the prepared pan. Using the tips of your fingers, press the pastry over the base. Grate the remaining pastry in and press into the edges of the tin, to the same thickness as the bottom. Rest in the refrigerator for at least 30 minutes.

4. Preheat the oven to 375°F (190°C). Bake the tart case, uncovered, for 15 minutes. Set aside to cool. Reduce the oven temperature to 350°F (180°C). Scatter one-third of the raspberries over the bottom of the tart case then spoon the almond mixture over the top. Bake for 30 minutes, or until just firm and golden brown. Allow to cool.

5. To serve, push indentations all over the surface with your fingertips, and fill with the rest of the raspberries. Slice and dust with icing sugar.

Lemon creams with poached cherries

Tasmanian dairy produce is just about the best you can get anywhere in the world, so why come all this way, and not take advantage of it? This dessert is a bit of a calorie killer but hey, what the hell. It's dead easy, but you'll need a thermometer. Use 2 lemons if you like a subtle lemon flavour, or 3 for more of a zing. I like using frozen sour cherries to cook with — fresh cherries should be eaten fresh.

SERVES 6

3½ cups	35% whipping cream	875 mL
	Finely grated rind and juice of 2–3 lemons	
6 oz	instant dissolving sugar	175 g

Poached cherries

	Finely grated rind of ½ orange	
7 fl oz	red wine (Shiraz or Cabernet Sauvignon)	200 mL
½	cinnamon stick	½
1	whole clove	1
1 tsp	instant dissolving sugar plus extra, if needed	5 mL
7 oz	frozen sour black cherries, defrosted	200 g

❶ In a saucepan, heat the cream to 160°F (70°C). Remove from the heat and cool to 150°F (65°C).

❷ Add the lemon rind, juice and sugar to the cream mixture, and mix well. Allow to cool, then pour into six 6-inch (175 mL) dariole moulds (cups or glasses will do if you don't have moulds*). Place on a tray and put in the refrigerator to set, about 4 hours.

❸ To poach the cherries: place the rind, wine, cinnamon, clove and sugar in a saucepan, and bring to a simmer. Add the cherries, bring to the boil, and taste for sweetness. If necessary, add a little more sugar to neutralise the tannin of the wine, while retaining some zing. Simmer for 5 minutes, then cool.

❹ When ready to serve, carefully up-end the moulds over serving plates and give them a shake; the creams should just slip out. If this proves difficult, run a small knife around the edge of the mould to release the cream and try again.

❺ Serve each lemon cream accompanied by 5–6 cherries. Drizzle a little of the syrup over each one.

* You can also make moulds from 3-inch (8-cm) diameter PVC pipe from a hardware store cut to depths of 1¼ inches (3 cm). Sand the edges and then seal the bottoms with plastic wrap.

Frozen berries with hot white chocolate sauce

I would usually advise people not to use frozen berries; however, with this chocolate sauce, the second the hot sauce and the frozen berries touch, the sauce solidifies making a lovely mound of chocolate-covered berries. The heat from the sauce also begins to break down the berries. It's hard to describe in words, but believe me it's worth trying.

SERVES 4

5 oz	fresh raspberries	150 g
5 oz	fresh blue berries	150 g
5 oz	fresh blackberries	150 g
1 cup	18% cream	250 mL
2	vanilla beans, split in half lengthways	2
8 oz	white chocolate, finely chopped	250 g

1. Spread the berries on a tray, making sure they are well spaced. Cover with plastic wrap and transfer to the freezer. Leave until frozen.

2. Place the cream and vanilla beans in a saucepan, and heat to just below simmering. Place the chocolate in a bowl, and strain the cream over the chocolate. Stir constantly until smooth.

3. Arrange the berries on a serving platter, and pour the hot sauce over the top. Serve at once.

Curtis Stone

Margaret River

Margaret River

Wino's, Waves, and Chardonnays

Ben O'Donoghue

Curtis and I lobbed into Perth, Western Australia, direct from London, bleary-eyed and jet-lagged. We're here because this is where I did most of my growing up. We're also here to check out what's been happening in the food scene. And to squeeze in a surf or two, something I don't get the chance to do as often as I'd like in Old Blighty. With this in mind, it made sense that we should drive straight to Margaret River, about three and a half hours south of Perth, famous (even in London) for its award-winning wines, gourmet foods, brilliant coastline, forests, and spectacular (although sometimes downright bloody dangerous) surf beaches.

The Margaret River region has had an interesting history, starting over a century ago producing timber. The massive karri and tuart hardwoods soar more than 200 feet (60 metres) into the sky, their gun-barrel-straight trunks were ideal for, among other things, the masts of giant sailing ships. In the early 1900s, logging and clearing had transformed a lot of the land from lush forest to dairy country. Beef farming followed shortly after. Today Margaret River is probably best known for its international award-winning wine industry which, surprisingly, did not start out until the early 1970s, making the winemakers' achievements even greater. Apparently, an agricultural scientist working for the State government researched the area and discovered that it had an almost identical micro-culture to the famous French wine-producing region of Bordeaux, so I guess it was inevitable that, unrestrained by centuries of unchanging and legislated techniques, it would end up rivaling them. I even have some Margaret River wines on the wine list in my restaurant. As well as being good wines, they remind me of home.

After the road trip from Perth, which passed without incident (except for a speeding ticket!), we drove along the main street of Margaret River, and decided to head for the 'main break,' where the river meets the sea. When we parked, the swell and the wind weren't working for us, so we headed a couple of miles south to a spot I knew as 'Grunters.' Just as we got there a whole busload of schoolkids arrived for their weekly surf lesson, so the traffic on the break was a little

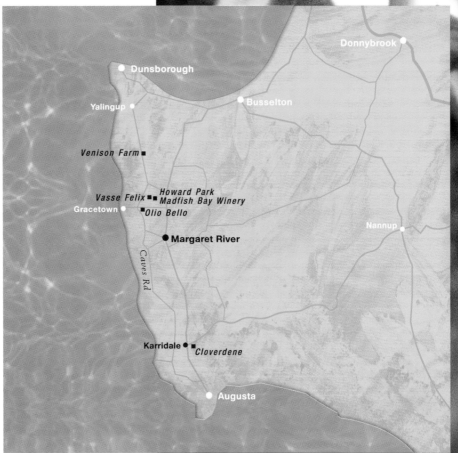

Dunsborough

Donnybrook

Yalingup

Busselton

Venison Farm ■

Howard Park
Vasse Felix ■ ■ Madfish Bay Winery
Gracetown ● ■ Olio Bello

● Margaret River

Nannup

Caves Rd

Karridale ● ■
Cloverdene

Augusta

like the Kings Road, Chelsea, on a Saturday morning. It's not good for the ego to get shown up by a bunch of pimply, pre-pubescent twelve-year-olds carving up the waves. We decided to go elsewhere.

From the cliff top we could see a nice break a little further south. There were only a few guys out, so we headed down. Curtis has got this 'Noah' (Noah's Ark= shark) phobia, so I dreamed up some stories about mates who'd been taken from this exact spot. He waxed the board for a little longer than normal while he slyly checked the waves for fins. A big pod of dolphins breaking the surface out the back of the waves made him look twice.

We pulled on our wetties, strapped on the leggies, and paddled out. Out the back of the breakers we said g'day to the other crew. Amazingly, among them was a bloke named Aaron Carr, whom I had done my apprenticeship with. I knew he was down this way, and was hoping to catch up. Knowing Aaron, the first place I should have thought to look was the surf. (If you think this sounds like a bit too much of a coincidence, we encountered an even better one. Later that day, Curtis called his brother Luke — who lives in Melbourne and whom he hasn't seen for three years — and when Curtis asked where he was, he said Margaret River. Unbelievably, Luke was a couple of miles away with his girlfriend.)

Anyway, as there's a fair bit of sitting around and waiting when you surf, we got to talking to these guys, and found they were all mostly in the food or wine business. It seems most of them are there for the surf first and the job second. Curtis and I said that if they scored us some produce, we'd knock up a meal. Aaron, who's head chef at Vasse Felix winery, said we could use his kitchen.

One of the other guys we met was Mike Gadd. He's an international winemaker, and owner of Wino's, a wine bar and restaurant in the main street. Wino's house wine, his award-winning current vintage red, is served on-tap from a keg! It's a damned good drop, too. Anyway, as Mike seems to know everyone and everything that goes on he said he'd show us around.

We decided to first check out Aaron's kitchen. He soon sorted us out with some duck breasts, great local asparagus, and some excellent Shiraz and

Chardonnay. On the way out, Curtis and I spotted this huge fig tree. It was chockers with ripe fruit, and Curtis, never one to miss out on an opportunity, suggested I back the truck up. By standing on the back seat, he was able to pick (or nick) a basketful of figs. (Stolen fruit is always the sweetest, I reckon!) The duck breasts and the figs gave Curtis an idea for a recipe; I was still looking.

Next morning we picked up Mike, who was a little quieter than usual. The night before had been the wake for Di Cullen, winemaker extraordinaire, and matriarch of the Margaret River region. The Cullen family were the first to plant vines in the region. I'm not certain if Mike's quieter demeanour was the result of his solemnity or the magnums of red that were brought up from the Cullens' cellar for the wake. A little of both, I suspect. Put that many winemakers and that much red together in one place and it's critical mass, party style.

He suggested one stop should be at Cloverdene, Trevor and Debbie Dennis's place in Karridale. As we drove into the property, about thirty plump guineafowl scattered, and a gang of kelpies, that quintessential Australian sheepdog, jumped enthusiastically alongside the car. Trev came in from checking a flock of sheep. He explained they had just started milking again — the sheep that is. A shearer by trade, Trevor loves sheep, and he and Debbie have combined that love with an interest in biodynamic and organic farming, and ended up with a business making sheep cheese. The traditionally inspired cheeses are full-flavoured — particularly impressive was an aged pecorino. Something to go with asparagus perhaps?

There was just time for a quick surf before we headed back to Vasse Felix to take over Aaron's kitchen. Prep for dinner came and went in a blur. When we were done, we were lucky enough to sit with our new mates out on the verandah overlooking the vineyards as a gentle sea breeze blew away the heat of the day. Curtis's brother and his girlfriend were also able to join us. David Birch, whom we'd met surfing, was still harvesting late into the night but sent along some wine anyway. Now that's the kind of friend I like!

We not only had some new friends to share the beautiful food and wonderful wine with, we had some old ones, too.

Poached asparagus

First, poach the eggs as these can be done in advance, kept in cold water and reheated for serving.

SERVES 4

4	*very fresh free-range eggs*	4
1 tsp	*white wine vinegar*	5 mL
2 tsp	*salt*	10 mL
12 oz	*asparagus*	375 g
3¹/₂ oz	*Parmigiano Reggiano or pecorino cheese, finely grated*	100 g
	Juice of 1 lemon	
7 fl oz	*extra-virgin olive oil*	200 mL
	Freshly ground black pepper	
1	*head celery, pale inner leaves only, coarsely chopped*	1
¹/₂ cup	*coarsely chopped fresh mint leaves*	125 mL

❶ Crack each egg into a cup. Fill a deep saucepan with water, and bring to the boil. Reduce to a simmer, and add the vinegar and 1 tsp (5 mL) salt. Stir with a spoon to make a whirlpool and drop an egg into the centre. Cook for 3–4 minutes, until the white is firm, and the yolk runny. Remove with a slotted spoon, and transfer to a bowl of cold water. Repeat with the remaining eggs.

❷ Bring a large saucepan of water to the boil, and add the remaining salt. Snap off the base of the asparagus spears where they become naturally tender, or trim, and peel the ends. Tie the spears into batches of equal thickness, and poach until tender, 2–4 minutes, according to their size. It is better if they are tender rather than crunchy. Discard the string.

❸ To make the dressing, place the cheese in a bowl, and add half the lemon juice. Mash with a spoon to form a paste. Gradually incorporate enough of the remaining lemon juice to give a smooth paste, that isn't too sharp in taste. Now stir in the oil in small amounts to make a creamy mayonnaise-like mixture. Season to taste with the black pepper. Alternatively, place dressing ingredients in a food processor, and whiz to form a smooth paste. The consistency should be runny, but not entirely liquid.

continued over...

4 To serve, gently lower the eggs into the asparagus cooking water to reheat. Toss the asparagus with half of the dressing, coating well. Place on serving plates. Using a slotted spoon, remove the eggs from the water, and place on top of the asparagus. Drizzle the remaining dressing over the eggs and around the plate, then sprinkle the celery and mint leaves on top. Finally, season with more black pepper.

Ben O'Donoghue

Creamy Parmesan and parsley polenta

Polenta is the Italian answer to mashed potato. It is a very versatile dish and can be used wet, like mashed potato, or it can be cooked a little longer and left to set. The polenta can then be cut and grilled, and served simply with a good Napoli sauce as a starter.

SERVES 4

5 cups	milk	1.25 L
1	small sprig fresh thyme	1
3	cloves garlic, peeled and crushed with the back of a knife	3
1	fresh bay leaf	1
4 oz	polenta (not instant)	125 g
2 tbsp	butter, softened	30 mL
2 oz	freshly grated Parmesan cheese	60 g
2 tsp	finely chopped fresh flat-leaf parsley	10 mL
	Freshly grated nutmeg	
	Salt and freshly ground black pepper	

1. Put the milk, thyme, garlic, and bay leaf in a saucepan, and bring to the near boil. Strain into a clean pan. Slowly whisk in the polenta. Place back on the heat and continue to whisk until it comes to the boil. Reduce the heat to very low and simmer, stirring often, for 1 hour. The polenta should resemble the consistency of mashed potato. Once it is cooked it will not have a floury taste.

2. Stir in the butter, Parmesan and parsley, and season with nutmeg, salt and pepper to taste.

Curtis Stone

Marinated salmon with oyster fritters, and a lemon and yoghurt dressing

Gravlax is originally a Scandinavian dish, which involves marinating salmon in a salty pickle, and pressing between 2 stones, to intensify the flavour. I don't use 2 stones but it's important to have a long thin knife to slice the salmon finely.

SERVES 4

½	leek, white part only	½
1	large shallot	1
½ cup	loosely packed fresh dillweed	125 mL
	Finely grated rind of 1 orange	
	Finely grated rind of 1 lemon	
3½ oz	sugar	100 g
3½ oz	sea salt	100 g
2 lb	side of fresh salmon	1 kg
¼ cup	Dijon mustard	50 mL
2½ cups	finely chopped fresh dillweed	625 mL

Dressing

3½ fl oz	plain yoghurt	100 mL
¼ cup	milk	50 mL
1 tbsp	freshly squeezed lemon juice	15 mL
	Salt and freshly ground black pepper	

Batter

7 fl oz	pilsner beer, at room temperature	200 mL
⅓ oz	fresh yeast	10 g
Pinch	instant dissolving sugar	Pinch
3½ oz	all-purpose flour	100 g
	Salt and freshly ground black pepper	
2 cups	vegetable oil for frying	500 mL
8	oysters, freshly opened	8
2–3 tbsp	all-purpose flour	30–45 mL

1. Place the leek, shallot, dillweed, orange and lemon rinds, sugar and salt in a food processor, and blitz well. Rub over both sides of the salmon, and wrap tightly in plastic wrap. Place on a tray, and put another tray on top. Weight this and transfer the lot to the refrigerator. Marinate for 24–48 hours.

2. Unwrap the salmon, thoroughly wash off the marinade with water, and pat dry with paper towels. Smear the side without skin with the mustard. Press the chopped dillweed onto the mustard. Slice the salmon into thin strips and arrange, overlapping, on 4 plates.

3. To make the dressing, whisk the yoghurt and milk together in a bowl, then while whisking constantly, gradually add the lemon juice. Season to taste with salt and pepper.

4. To make the batter, place the beer, yeast and sugar in a bowl, and leave in a warm place for 10 minutes. Whisk in the flour gradually, and season with salt and pepper.

5. Heat the oil in a small saucepan over moderately high heat. Dust the oysters with the flour, then dip into the batter. Fry the oysters, a few at a time, in the hot oil until golden, about 1–2 minutes. Drain on paper towels. Place 2 oysters on each plate and drizzle the dressing over the salmon for serving.

Curtis Stone

Crab and chili tagliatelle

Crabmeat is a perfect example of seafood that needs to be kept simple. The flavour works well with a hint of chili and a little bit of citrus. As the crabmeat has been cooked before it is picked from the shell, it only needs to be reheated in the sauce, making this a very quick dish to prepare.

SERVES 4

5	plum tomatoes	5
1 tbsp	olive oil	15 ml
2	shallots, finely diced	2
3	cloves garlic, minced	3
1	bird's-eye chili, finely chopped	1
7 oz	crabmeat	200 g
3½ fl oz	dry white wine	100 mL
1 lb	fresh tagliatelle (or 12 oz [375 g] dried)	500 g
4 tbsp	butter	60 mL
¼ cup	water	50 mL
2 tbsp	finely chopped fresh flat-leaf parsley	30 mL
2 tbsp	extra-virgin olive oil	30 mL
1 tbsp	freshly squeezed lemon juice	15 mL
4	sprigs fresh chervil to garnish	4

1. Core the tomatoes, cut a cross on the opposite end, then plunge into boiling water, and blanch for 12–15 seconds. Remove with a slotted spoon, and cool in ice water. Peel, and squeeze out any excess moisture, then dice. Reserve.

2. Heat the olive oil in a skillet. Add the shallots, garlic and chili, and cook over moderately low heat until soft, but not browned, 1–2 minutes. Add the crabmeat and cook for 30 seconds. Add the white wine, increase the heat, and stir to deglaze. The sauce will reduce while the pasta is cooking.

3. Cook the tagliatelle in boiling salted water for 1–2 minutes, or according to the manufacturer's instructions. Melt the butter with the water in a large saucepan. Drain the pasta and place in the pan of butter and water. Toss to coat well. Add half the parsley to the pasta, tossing the remainder in with the crab sauce. Stir in the reserved tomatoes, the extra-virgin olive oil and the lemon juice.

4. Take a quarter of the pasta and twist it around a roasting fork. Place it on a warmed pasta bowl and gently slide the fork out, leaving a spiral. Repeat with the remaining pasta. Spoon the sauce around the outside and garnish each serve with a sprig of chervil.

Curtis Stone

Peppered duck breast, poached balsamic figs, and garlic crisps with jus gras

Duck is a lovely rich meat. The classic 'Duck à la orange' works so well because the acidity of the citrus fruit cuts through the richness of the duck. In this dish I use instead the acidity of the balsamic. It's important to blanch the slices of garlic so that the flavour is not overpowering.

SERVES 4

3 tbsp	coarsely ground black pepper	45 mL
4	duck breasts, weighing about 7 oz (200 g) each	4
1 cup	vegetable oil for frying	250 mL
4	ripe figs	4
1 cup	balsamic vinegar	250 mL
12	cloves garlic, very thinly sliced	12
4 cups	milk	1 L
	Sea salt	
2 cups	picked watercress leaves	500 mL

1. Preheat the oven to 400°F (200°C). Place the pepper on a plate and firmly press the duck breasts skin-side down into it.

2. Heat 1 tbsp (15 mL) oil in a skillet with a heatproof handle. Fry the duck breasts, skin-side down, over medium heat until golden brown, about 4–5 minutes. They should be cooked on the skin-side only to prevent them drying out. Transfer the pan to the oven for 5 minutes. Remove the duck from the oven and allow to rest for 3–5 minutes.

3. Prick the figs with a skewer, then place the figs and balsamic vinegar in a small saucepan. Heat gently for 4–5 minutes, then remove from the heat.

4. Place the garlic in a small saucepan and add one-third of the milk. Bring to the near boil. Strain and return the garlic to the saucepan. Repeat this procedure twice. Pat the garlic dry with paper towels. Heat the remaining oil in a small skillet and fry the garlic until golden brown, 4–5 minutes. Drain on paper towels and season with salt.

continued over...

Curtis Stone

Peppered duck breast, poached balsamic figs, and garlic crisps with jus gras, continued...

⑤ To serve, slice each breast into 5 medallions and arrange in a semi-circle on 4 plates. Slice the figs in half and sit behind the duck. Place a small bunch of watercress and some garlic crisps on either side of the fig, and drizzle a little jus gras over each breast.

Jus gras

YIELDS ABOUT 2/3 CUP (150 ML)

2 lb	chicken wings	1 kg
1/3 cup	vegetable oil	75 mL
4 cups	chicken stock	1 L
2 3/4 oz	shallots, sliced	75 g
3	cloves garlic, crushed with the back of a knife	3
5	white peppercorns	5
1	sprig fresh thyme	1
3	fresh bay leaves	3

① Chop each chicken wing into 3. Heat the oil in a heavy-based saucepan over high heat and brown the wings, 4–5 minutes. Remove the wings from the pan, drain the oil and return the wings to the pan.

② Add the stock, shallots, garlic, peppercorns, thyme and bay leaves, and slowly bring to the boil. Simmer over very low heat, uncovered, for 2 hours, or until the stock is rich and reduced to about 2/3 (150 mL) cup.

③ Strain into a bowl. Place a heavy pan on top of the wings to squeeze out all the juice, and leave for 30 minutes. Discard the bones. Pass the stock through muslin. If necessary, get rid of the excess fat by chilling the stock; the fat will solidify on top and can be easily taken off.

Curtis Stone

Venison wrapped in coppa di forma with porcini mushrooms

Get your butcher and local deli person to do the hard yards by trimming the venison and slicing the coppa di forma. It's good to know the size of the venison loin before buying the coppa di forma, so go to the butcher first. The deli can then overlap the slices of coppa di forma on waxed paper, to a size large enough to cover (roughly 3 times as wide, and as long as) the meat.

SERVES 4

1/2 oz	dried porcini	15 g
3 1/2 oz	unsalted butter, softened	100 g
8 oz	field mushrooms, sliced	250 g
2	cloves garlic, finely chopped	2
	Salt and freshly ground black pepper	
1 1/2 oz	fresh bread crumbs	45 g
1/2	bunch fresh thyme	1/2
1/2	bunch fresh rosemary	1/2
1/2	bunch fresh sage	1/2
2 lb	trimmed venison loin	1 kg
8 oz	coppa di forma (approx, see above)	250 g
1 cup	red wine, such as Shiraz	250 mL

1 Soak the porcini in boiling water for 10 minutes. Drain, rinse under cold water and squeeze dry. Melt 2 tbsp (30 mL) butter in a skillet and add the mushrooms. Cook until coloured, then add the porcini and garlic. Cook, stirring, for 2–3 minutes, until moist but not dry. Season with salt and pepper, and stir in the bread crumbs. Set aside to cool.

2 Pick the leaves off the thyme, rosemary, and sage. Reserve half. Chop the remainder, and sprinkle over the venison with a little pepper.

3 Lie the paper carrying the overlapping slices of coppa di forma on a flat surface. Place the venison on top, end to end with the coppa di forma. Spread the mushroom mixture along the length of the meat. Starting from 1 side and using the paper for leverage, roll the coppa di forma around the meat to form a sausage. Tie with string in several places to secure.

continued opposite...

4 In a non-stick skillet large enough to fit the meat (if this size is unavailable, cut the roll into 4 even portions), melt 3 tbsp (45 mL) butter. When it starts to foam, add the venison and fry over gentle heat for 12–15 minutes, until crisp and brown on all sides*. Add the reserved herbs and fry until crisp. Transfer the meat and herbs to a plate, cover with foil and leave to rest.

5 Pour the wine into the skillet, increase the heat and reduce by half. Turn off the heat and add the last of the butter. Swirl until melted to give a sauce with an intense wine flavour. Slice the venison and serve with the sauce and pot-roasted baby turnips.

* Venison should be served rare to medium but if you like it well done just cook it for 10 minutes longer.

Pot-roasted turnips

I love pot-roasted baby turnips with venison, but you could serve your own favourite vegetable with it. They are equally as good with lamb.

SERVES 4

24	baby turnips	24
16	cloves garlic, peeled	16
	Salt and freshly ground black pepper	
2 tbsp	butter	30 mL
1 tsp	white wine vinegar	5 mL
2 tbsp	finely chopped fresh flat-leaf parsley	30 mL

1 Bring a saucepan of water to the boil and add the turnips, garlic and 1/2 tsp (2 mL) salt. Simmer gently for about 15 minutes, until the turnips are tender. Drain. Add the butter to the pan and heat gently until foaming. Return the turnips and garlic in a single layer and cook over a gentle heat for 5–10 minutes, until golden brown. Add the vinegar and parsley, and season to taste with salt and pepper. Serve immediately.

Sparkling strawberry wine jellies

SERVES 6

3¹/₂ oz	instant dissolving sugar	100 g
3 cups	strawberry sparkling wine or sparkling rosé, chilled	750 mL
6	leaves gelatin	6
1 lb	ripe strawberries	500 g
1 tbsp	finely chopped fresh borage or mint	15 mL
2 tbsp	peeled, seeded and finely chopped cucumber, white flesh only	30 mL
1 tbsp	icing sugar	15 mL
	Crème fraîche or sour cream to serve	

① Combine the sugar and ¹/₃ cup (75 mL) wine in a medium saucepan. Stir gently over low heat to dissolve the sugar. Soak the gelatin in cold water until soft, then squeeze dry. Add to the saucepan, and stir until dissolved.

② Reserve half a punnet of strawberries for a coulis and 6 strawberries to decorate. Core and roughly chop the remainder. Place in a bowl with the borage or mint and cucumber, and lightly toss to combine. Distribute between 6 cappuccino cups or six 6-inch (175-mL) dariole moulds.

③ Stir the remaining wine into the gelatin mixture and gently pour over the fruit. Place on a small tray for easy handling and put into the freezer to chill rapidly. When they begin to set, transfer to the refrigerator to fully set.

④ To make the coulis, purée the reserved half punnet of strawberries with the icing sugar and pass through a sieve.

⑤ To serve, place the moulds into hot water for a couple of seconds to loosen the jellies, then turn out onto a plate. Serve with the coulis, crème fraîche or sour cream and the reserved strawberries.

Mascarpone and raspberry crème brûlée

This is a sweet creamy classic from France. I love mascarpone cheese and I think the tartness of the raspberries breaks up the consistency a little. If you don't have a blowtorch you can caramelize the sugar under a hot grill.

SERVES 4

3 tbsp	milk	45 mL
14 fl oz	35% whipping cream	450 mL
1	vanilla bean, split in half lengthways	1
3	free-range egg yolks	3
1	free-range egg	1
1/3 cup	instant dissolving sugar	75 mL
1 cup	mascarpone cheese	250 mL
12	raspberries	12
2 tbsp	demerara sugar or brown sugar	30 mL

① Place the milk, cream and vanilla in a medium saucepan and slowly bring to the near boil.

② In a clean saucepan, lightly whisk the egg yolks, egg and sugar together until creamy. Gradually add the mascarpone, whisking constantly.

③ Pour the milk over the egg mixture and stir to combine. Place over low heat and whisk constantly until the mixture thickens and coats the back of a wooden spoon. Strain into a jug.

④ Place 3 raspberries in the bottom of 4 thick martini glasses. Pour the crème mixture over the top. Transfer to the refrigerator to set overnight.

⑤ Sprinkle the surfaces evenly with the demerara sugar. Use a blowtorch or preheat the griller to hot and place the crèmes under the heat until the sugar melts and caramelizes.

⑥ Serve when cooled a little.

Curtis Stone

Bellarine Peninsula

Bellarine Peninsula

Mussels, Zen, and Spice Girl

Curtis Stone

The Bellarine Peninsula, just a sixty-minute drive from Melbourne, extends from Geelong to Queenscliffe, and down to Torquay, just before Bells Beach on the Surf Coast. The peninsula offers both protected bay outlooks and beaches, as well as spectacular ocean vistas and excellent surf. This is where I did some of my growing up.

So what can I tell you about my peninsula? Well, the Geelong region grew prosperous through servicing the needs of the wool-growers and squatters who thrived around the peninsula area and into the hinterland in the mid-nineteenth century. Queenscliffe, at the western edge of the entrance to the massive Port Phillip Bay, initially became best known as the home of the pilot service, which from 1838 guided ships through the reefs and the narrow entrance into the bay. Because of the dangerous tides at the entrance it became known as 'the rip.' In the 1850s a lighthouse and lifeboat rescue service were added. This coincided with a massive increase in the number of ships arriving due to the discovery of gold not far inland at Ballarat and Bendigo. Ships, filled to overflowing with hopefuls from all over the world, landed almost every day. In the 1800s, for some reason fearing an attack from the Russians, massive cannons were installed at the western and eastern entrance to the bay. The attack never came, and the cannons were rarely, if ever, fired in anger. In the late 1800s, holiday-makers sailed across the bay in ferries and boats from Melbourne to holiday at Queenscliffe. Many beautiful, grand Victorian hotels and guesthouses sprang up, and are still patronised to this day.

While little appears to have changed in Queenscliffe, west along the coast through Barwon Heads, and down to Torquay much has changed as holiday-makers, and especially surfers, take advantage of the spectacular coastline and consistent surf. The peninsula today has also become a magnet for foodies, gourmet producers, and quality wines. The mild climate makes the region ideal for growing all manner of produce. There's local mussels, shellfish such as scallops and lobster, plus fish from Port Phillip Bay and the wild seas of Bass Strait. In addition,

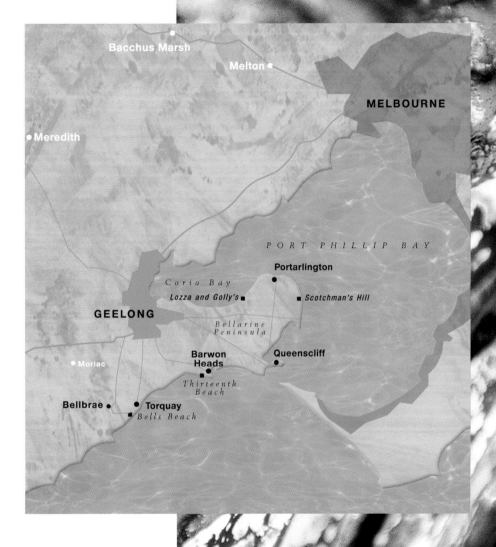

Bacchus Marsh

Melton

MELBOURNE

Meredith

PORT PHILLIP BAY

Portarlington

Corio Bay

Lozza and Golly's ■

■ *Scotchman's Hill*

GEELONG

*Bellarine
Peninsula*

**Barwon
Heads** ●

Queenscliff

*Thirteenth
Beach*

Moriac

Bellbrae ●

● **Torquay**
■ *Bells Beach*

there is beef and lamb, rabbit, duck, poultry, game and cheeses, even buffalo mozzarella. Plus there are some fantastic vineyards that produce some of my favourite wines. Let's take a short tour of some of what we discovered.

First, family. We called in to see my mother Lorraine (Lozza) and Golly. (His real name's Shane but my brother, Luke, and I have always called him Golly because he used to have thick curly black hair.) In Lozza and Golly's back-yard there is a large and lush herb garden, as well as the last of some fresh rhubarb and seasonal vegetables. I introduced Bender to Donald and Daisy, the pet ducks. The ducks sat unperturbed on their pond (well, actually, bath-tub set in the ground) while I stirred Lozza about how good they'd taste roasted and served in a red wine jus …

What I observed about this homecoming was that it is not only the young or the herbal types living in Nimbin, Margaret River and so on, who are into recycling, rediscovering, and redefining their lives. There was evidence of a quiet revolution everywhere — Lozza and Golly are living a more natural and simpler existence with their chooks and ducks providing free-range eggs, and an organic herb and veggie patch I'd kill for. Golly puts his boat into the bay at the foot of our street to catch fresh fish. In some aspects, they're almost self-sufficient.

After dropping in on Lozza and Golly, Bender, and I headed out for the surf. While Bender thinks that Margaret River is the epitome of the surfing scene, I wanted to show him my neck of the woods. Bells Beach is a little out of my league (the best surfers in the world don't come here to compete in the Ripcurl Masters for nothing), but Thirteenth Beach about fifteen minutes from Lozza's is always consistent, and offers a wave on most days. On the day we went it wasn't as big as it can get, but it did offer a fun time in the waves so we grabbed the boards and headed on in.

As usual a good wave acts like a magnet, and we headed over to where a group had already gathered. On the peninsula it's not unusual to drive along the parking areas and see pick-up after pick-up parked side-by-side. The locals know that on a big surf day, you won't be able to get a tradesman for love or money. That's the situation for many similar seaside towns. In management jargon, I think that's called prioritizing. I'd love to have that attitude, but I enjoy what I do so much that I guess all that other stuff will have to stay on the backburner for a while.

Out in the surf there was a whole bunch of different people. After we'd said g'day, we ended up talking to a bunch of foodies who all seemed to have taken a leaf out of the tradesmen's books. We caught a few waves over the next hour or so, and told them we're back home for Lozza's wedding anniversary. Grant Hutchins of The Heads restaurant immediately offered the use of his kitchen, and part of the restaurant for the party. As they have a dishwasher, and Mum doesn't, we thought this was a good idea. The restaurant was perfect — casual and stylish — and, perched over the river, it had a view to die for.

Apparently The Heads is quite famous because it was Diver Dan's home in the television programme *Sea Change*. This didn't have any impact on Bender and me as we've been away for around six years each, and had completely missed the programme. We later found out that Lozza loved the show, and loved the idea of having the celebration there. We now had to source some local produce. Where better to start than with the people we met surfing?

In the small town of Bellbrae (just north of Bells Beach), Albie Cachia and her husband Gerrard run The Screaming Seeds Spice Company. Walk inside and the air is thick with the aromas of exciting blends. Albie constantly applies her Mediterranean instincts to guide her while trying out new spice combinations. She is also using Australian native outback blends, which include lemon myrtle and Dorrigo pepper. Albie and Gerrard are not afraid to experiment and invent new taste sensations.

Zen's makes largely Italian-style breads. Danny Zen's ciabatta are infused with olives, basil or roasted vegetables. The bakery is a family affair. Father Giannni came to the region from Padua in the Veneto, and started the Belmont bakery almost fifty years ago, bringing the Italian traditions with him. Danny now bakes the bread while sister Gabrielle runs the front of house.

Danny suggested we call into a local provender, Warren and Hutch, so named because the owners, Sarah and Jane, had originally owned a rabbit farm of the same name. Jane had previously attended a Cordon Bleu school in England, and Sarah had been involved in promoting Australian produce throughout the UK — so food and wine are definitely in their blood.

They met us at the door wearing starched aprons and warm smiles. Inside the store, Bender and I got into a conversation about what was fresh. Bender chose some plump free-range hens for the party, which he intended to prepare with Albie's spices. Sarah and Jane know everything about everything food-wise, and who does what in the region.

They mentioned that Bob Grant was worth a visit. He's an apiarist, but not a typical one. While many of his hives are out in the countryside, he has three hives set out in the backyard of his welding shop. Bob explained that the suburbs are one of the best places for hives because bees need flowers, and suburban gardens are chock-full of flowering plants, shrubs, and trees. Another surprising fact: pure honey is a powerful antibiotic. In countries such as Russia, honey has been used as a medication for centuries. This reminded me of a conversation we'd had with Baamba in Broome about how traditional Aboriginals collected bush honey to treat cuts or scratches. Bob also told us another fact: if the seal on a honeycomb is unbroken it can keep for over a century! Isn't nature full of surprises?

Apparently the honey industry in Australia is unique compared to the northern hemisphere where almost all the honey production is from ground and meadow flowers. Here, due to the prolifically flowering gums and native plants, such as grevillia, almost all our honey is from flowering trees that are high in pollen content and goodness.

Earlier, Lozza had suggested if we wanted fresh mussels we should get along and see Wayne Senior (known as Mr Mussels) and Wayne Junior on the Portarlington Pier. On the peninsula most things are no further than ten or fifteen minutes apart, and a short drive later we are at the pier in Portarlington. Wayne and Wayne were just preparing to go and harvest some of their mussels so we hitched a ride. We figured we wouldn't be able to get mussels any fresher if we pulled them ourselves.

As baby hatchlings, mussels are funneled into a stocking-like casing (similar to making sausages) where a long rope runs through the centre from top to bottom. The casing holds the mussels against the rope long enough for the mussels to attach themselves by their own foot. There they remain for the rest of their lives, growing plump and tender. The ropes of mussels are hung from long lines between buoys just a five-minute boat ride out into Corio Bay. Bender and I pulled some in ourselves. It's a completely natural way of farming — wild product with no messing about or adding anything unnatural. The mussels live in the clean tidal water and filter-feed naturally. When they are ready, they are harvested and can be on the table in just a few hours.

On the way back to the restaurant we called into Scotchman's Hill winery, which has been making wines since the mid 1800s. The winery sits proud on a hill overlooking Corio Bay where Melbourne city can be seen on the other side of the bay. We took some of their Cabernet Sauvignon and Chardonnay for the guests.

Ben and I headed back to Grant's restaurant and started to cook. And it wasn't long before I found out something I hadn't suspected about my mother before now — she's a dirty rotten sneak. I reckon of all the people in the world, you really should be able to trust your mates and your mum.

The reason (I thought) Bender and I were in the Bellarine Peninsula was to cook a special meal to celebrate Lozza and Golly's wedding anniversary. Mum had suggested it, I had gone along with it, and Bender had agreed to help out. Lozza had told me that she was inviting a lot of her new friends who've moved into the neighbourhood, and that I wouldn't know anyone, but it would be good for me to meet them. Occasionally I'd pop out of the kitchen to check on the arrival of these guests, but even as the appointed hour drew near no one had arrived. I should have smelt a rat, but being the honest, believable, and, as it turned out, gullible soul that I am, I was completely in the dark.

Eventually Mum announced that all her friends were there, and, not wishing to overcook the meal, Bender and I plated-up and headed into the restaurant to serve. But, rather than a whole table of Mum's cronies there sat just about all of my best friends, none of whom I'd been able to catch up with since I'd been in Australia. They had flown in from Queensland and Tasmania; and some had driven from the country, one had even cut short footy training. (Considering he was voted Best on Ground two days later, perhaps he should try that more often!)

It was a brilliant surprise and, as it turned out, everyone, even Bender and Grant, the restaurant owner, had been in on it. I did feel like an idiot, but a happy one. Great food. Great friends. Even when you've been away for almost six years, your mates are your mates for life. What else is there?

Well, there's always footy, and after another kick in the backyard with Bender, I snuck off to watch my brother play for his Aussie Rules amateur team, East Keilor. It's great to catch up with family and friends, and experience the simple pleasures — like having a beer at the footy with your brother. Something I don't get to do as often as I'd like.

Buffalo mozzarella, fava bean, mint, and arugula salad

I cannot think of anything I would rather eat during summer than this beautiful salad. It captures the freshness that represents everything about that season to me. As an option you can shave some pecorino cheese over the salad at the end to garnish, but I find the pale green, white and jagged dark green of the arugula appealing enough.

SERVES 4–6

10 oz	*shelled small fava beans**	*300 g*
	Salt	
2³/₄ oz	*pecorino cheese, freshly grated*	*75 g*
2 tbsp	*finely chopped fresh mint leaves*	*30 mL*
	Juice of 1 lemon	
	Freshly ground black pepper	
¹/₃ cup	*extra-virgin olive oil*	*75 mL*
3	*fresh buffalo mozzarella balls, weighing about 8 oz (250 g)***	*3*
2 cups	*loosely packed wild arugula*	*500 mL*
2 tbsp	*fresh mint leaves, torn if large*	*30 mL*

1 Place the fava beans and a little salt in a mortar, and smash to a rough, chunky paste. Add the pecorino cheese, half the chopped mint, and three-quarters of the lemon juice. Season to taste and toss to combine. Add enough olive oil, about 3 tbsp (45 mL), to make the mixture loose and wet.

2 Break the mozzarella into pieces, and place on a serving plate. Top with half of the fava bean mixture. Combine the arugula and torn mint with the remaining chopped mint, lemon juice and olive oil, and scatter over the mozzarella. Dress with the remaining fava bean mixture and black pepper.

As the fava beans are uncooked in this salad, only those that are fresh, young and small should be used. If unavailable, substitute with 1 lb (500 g) mature or frozen ones. These will need to be blanched for 1 minute, and shelled.

*** The equivalent weight of bocconcini (cow milk mozzarella) can be substituted.*

Marinated mussel salad

Curtis reckons the mussels in Port Phillip Bay are the best in Australia and, you know, he was close. It doesn't matter where the best mussels come from, just get the freshest ones you can find. If they're closed and heavy then they're alive, and if they smell good, and don't float in water, you're pretty well onto some fresh mussels. Mussels that are dead or that have been out of water for too long can be bloody lethal. This salad is ideal for a hot summer's lunch, starter or as part of a barbecue spread.

SERVES 4–6

4 lb	live fresh black mussels	2 kg
1 lb	mixed fresh tomatoes (red and yellow cherry, vine-ripened, green stripy)	500 g
	Salt and freshly ground black pepper	
1	clove garlic, thinly sliced	1
1	bunch fresh coriander	1
3 1/2 fl oz	ponzu sauce*	100 mL
1/2 tsp	peeled and minced fresh ginger	2 mL
1 tbsp	grated palm sugar (jaggery)	30 mL
2–3	green chilies, deseeded and sliced into thin strips	2–3
7 oz	honeydew melon, peeled and cubed	200 g

1. To clean the mussels, pull off the hairy beard, then rinse in cold water. Discard any mussels that float. Heat a heavy-based saucepan over high heat, then add just enough mussels to cover the base. Splash a little water over the top, and quickly cover with the lid. When they have opened, remove, and drain in a colander. Discard any that have not opened. Repeat this process until all the mussels are cooked. Allow to cool.

2. Extract the mussels from the shell and reserve, discarding the shells. Cut the tomatoes as you please; the smaller ones in half, larger ones into chunks or irregular shapes. Place in a large bowl, season with salt and pepper, and add the garlic.

3. Finely chop the coriander roots, and combine with the ponzu sauce, ginger and palm sugar, mixing well. Pour over the tomatoes, and add the reserved mussels. Taste for salt and pepper, and gently toss. Rest in the refrigerator for at least 2 hours.

4. Add the coriander leaves, chili and melon, and gently toss. Serve either as 1 big salad, or individually plated.

* To make the ponzu sauce, combine 2 tsp (10 mL) rice vinegar, 3 tbsp (45 mL) lime juice, 2 tsp (10 mL) mirin, 2 tbsp (30 mL) dashi and 3 tbsp (45 mL) soy sauce. Leave in the refrigerator overnight before use.

Spiced mussel and saffron soup

This is a soup that I picked up from the master, Marco Pierre White. I have altered it slightly but it is very much his creation. Don't worry about throwing away the mussels after you strain the soup. You have cooked all the flavour and juice out of them, so you are not wasting food — better yet, if you have a cat you will be a popular person.

SERVES 6

¼ cup	butter, softened	50 mL
1	onion, thinly sliced	1
1	stalk celery, thinly sliced	1
1	leek, thinly sliced	1
1 tsp	curry powder	5 mL
1 tsp	cayenne pepper	5 mL
2	fresh bay leaves	2
1	sprig fresh thyme	1
¼ tsp	saffron threads	1 mL
5½ lb	mussels, scrubbed and debearded	2.5 kg
3 cups	dry white wine	750 mL
2 cups	fish stock	500 mL
14 fl oz	18% cream	450 mL
	Salt and freshly ground black pepper	

1. Melt the butter in a large saucepan, then add the onion, celery, leek, curry powder, cayenne pepper, bay leaves, thyme, and saffron. Cook over low heat for 5–6 minutes, bleeding colour from the saffron.

2. Once the vegetables are soft, add the mussels, give them a good stir, and cover the saucepan. Cook until opened, about 1 minute. Discard those that haven't opened, and reserve 12–18 (depending on their size) to garnish. Add the wine, bring to the boil over high heat and cook for 8–10 minutes. Add the fish stock, and return to the boil. Reduce heat to low and simmer for 10 minutes. Add the cream and return to the near boil.

3. Strain the soup through a colander, then strain through a sieve lined with muslin. Season to taste with salt and pepper. Extract the meat from most of the mussels, and discard the shells; retain some in their shells to garnish the soup. To serve, ladle the soup into bowls and add the mussels.

Curtis Stone

Spaghettini vongole

This recipe originates from the south of Italy where the clams are wonderful. In Australia we are privileged to have access to some of the best seafood in the world, so we should take advantage of it. Serve with some crusty bread, so you can sop up the sauce.

SERVES 4

10 oz	dried spaghettini	300 g
	Sea salt	
2 tbsp	olive oil	30 mL
1	shallot, finely chopped	1
2	bird's-eye chilies, deseeded and finely chopped	2
2	cloves garlic, minced	2
1¼ lb	fresh clams (vongole)	625 g
¼ cup	dry white wine	50 mL
8	cherry tomatoes	8
1 tbsp	tapenade*	15 mL
1 tbsp	baby capers	15 mL
1½ oz	anchovies, finely chopped	45 g
½ cup	chopped fresh flat-leaf parsley	125 mL
⅓ cup	extra-virgin olive oil	75 mL
	Juice of 1 lemon	
	freshly ground black pepper	
⅓ cup	butter	75 mL
¼ cup	water	50 mL
4	sprigs fresh chervil to garnish	4

❶ Preheat the oven to 425°F (220°C). Bring a large saucepan of water to the boil. Add the spaghettini, a big pinch of salt and 1 tbsp (15 mL) olive oil. Cook for 6 minutes, or until al dente.

❷ Meanwhile, heat 2 tsp (10 mL) olive oil in a large saucepan over medium heat, add the shallot and chilies. Fry without browning for 30 seconds. Add the garlic, stir for 10 seconds, then add the clams and wine. Immediately cover and shake the pan. Cook for 1½ minutes.

❸ Place the tomatoes on a baking tray and drizzle with the remaining olive oil. Place in the oven for 5–6 minutes or until they start to burst.

❹ Once the clams start to open, add the tapenade, capers, anchovies and half the parsley. Shake the pan to ensure that everything is well mixed. Remove from the heat and stir in the extra-virgin olive oil and lemon juice. Season to taste with pepper.

continued opposite...

continued opposite...

* Tapenade can be purchased at delicatessens and large supermarkets.

Curtis Stone

5 Heat the butter and water in a saucepan. Drain the pasta and mix in the butter and water emulsion. Add the remaining parsley. Curl a quarter of the pasta around a roasting fork. When it is tightly in place, gently ease the spiral of pasta into the centre of a serving bowl. Repeat with the remaining pasta. Arrange the clams around the pasta and drizzle over the sauce. Place the tomatoes on the side of each bowl, and garnish with a sprig of chervil. Serve at once.

Curtis Stone

Spiced smoky barbecued chicken with a tomato and garlic relish

I developed this recipe for my kettle barbecue. I love the flavours that it imparts to food, and the social theatre that is imparted by this recipe will leave your friends with no doubt as to your creative finesse. The combination of smoke and spice is one that appears across cultures from the Caribbean to Coogee beach. You can use any type of spice combination that rocks your boat. We were lucky enough to come across a great spice shop in Bellbrae, and I could not resist their Kashmir-inspired curry mixture.

SERVES 4

2	cloves garlic, peeled and coarsely chopped	2
	Sea salt	
	Finely grated rind and juice of 2 lemons	
2 tbsp	Kashmiri spice mixture, or good-quality curry powder	30 mL
1	dried bird's-eye chili, deseeded and crushed	1
1/3 cup	olive oil	75 mL
	Freshly ground black pepper	
3 lb	organic chicken	1.5 kg
2	bunches fresh rosemary	2
1–2	bunches fresh bay leaves	1–2
2	bunches fresh thyme	2

1 Smash the garlic with a little salt in a mortar. Add the rind and half of the lemon juice. Add the spice mixture, chili, oil and black pepper to taste. Mix to a moist paste, adding a little more oil if necessary. This step can also be done in a mini food processor.

2 Remove the excess fat from inside the chicken. Starting from the tail end, carefully separate the skin from the meat by sliding your hand under the breast skin and gently lifting. Being careful not to break the skin, use scissors to snip the membrane that runs along the centre breast. Push the spice paste into the cavity you have made between the meat and skin and smear it over the meat.

3 Preheat a kettle or covered barbecue. When the coals have just turned an ashen white colour but are still whole, place the chicken breast-up directly onto the rack and season well with pepper. Close the lid and cook until the chicken starts to colour, 5–7 minutes. Remove the chicken and reduce the heat to low.

continued opposite...

4 Make a bed on the rack using the rosemary, bay leaves and thyme. Place the chicken breast-up on top. Drizzle the remaining lemon juice over the chicken and replace the lid; the herbs will start to smoke. Keep the lid on and cook for 40–45 minutes, or until the chicken juices run clear when the base of the leg is pieced. Don't open the lid too often, or you will lose the smoke. Allow to rest for 10–15 minutes before tucking in.

Spicy barbecued tomato and garlic relish

MAKES 1½–2 CUPS

5	long cayenne chillies	5
10	small or 5 large Asian shallots, unpeeled	10
10	cloves garlic, unpeeled	10
10	large cherry tomatoes	10
1 tbsp	red wine vinegar (approx)	15 mL
1 tbsp	olive oil (approx)	15 mL
	Salt and freshly ground black pepper	

1 Heat the barbecue to hot. Prick the chilies with a fork and char-grill until the skin blackens and blisters. When cool, peel and deseed.

2 Place the shallots and garlic cloves on the barbecue and cook over medium heat until soft. Don't worry if they turn black on the outside because you will be using only the soft inside flesh. Char-grill the tomatoes until soft and the skin splits.

3 Squeeze the soft flesh from the shallots, garlic and tomatoes into a mortar. Add the chilies and pound into a coarse relish. Add enough vinegar and oil to give a good relish consistency, then season with salt and pepper. This step can be done in a mini food processor. Store in the refrigerator, covered, for up to 1 week.

Ben O'Donoghue

Roast saddle of rabbit with baby leeks and asparagus

My uncle used to take my brother and me hunting for rabbits when we were kids. Wild rabbits are usually smaller, and the meat is a little tougher, so they can be trickier to cook. Tame or domestic rabbits are quite tender, and are relatively inexpensive. If you have not tried them, have a go — roast the saddles, and braise the legs.

SERVES 4

4	small rabbits, each weighing about 2 lb (1 kg), cleaned	4
2 tbsp	olive oil	30 mL
2	shallots, chopped	2
1	sprig fresh thyme	1
3	fresh bay leaves	3
8 cups	chicken stock	2 L
1 tbsp	35% whipping cream	15 mL
2 tbsp	cold butter, cubed	30 mL
	Salt and freshly ground black pepper	
20	spears asparagus, trimmed*	20
20	baby leeks, trimmed*	20

* Trim the asparagus and leeks to a similar size.

1 Remove the legs from the rabbits and chop them into 4 pieces using a cleaver or poultry shears. Heat 1 tbsp (15 mL) oil in a heavy-based saucepan and brown the legs over a moderately high heat. Pour off the fat. Add the shallots, thyme and bay leaves and cook for 3–5 minutes. Add the stock, increase the heat and stir to deglaze the pan.

2 Reduce the heat and simmer, uncovered, until reduced by three-quarters, about 40 minutes. Strain into a smaller saucepan. Add the cream and simmer gently for 2–3 minutes. Add the butter, cube by cube, whisking well after each addition, until the butter melts. Season to taste and keep warm.

3 Preheat the oven to 400°F (200°C). Remove the belly flaps from the rabbits and reserve. Heat the remaining oil in a cast-iron or flameproof roasting pan and fry the saddles over a high heat until golden brown on all sides. Push them to one side and spread out the belly flaps in the pan. Place the saddles on top and transfer to the oven. Roast for 5 minutes. Remove from the pan and rest for 5 minutes.

continued over...

Curtis Stone

4 Cut the belly flaps into thin strips and return to the hot pan. Fry over a high heat until crispy. Drain on paper towels.

5 Bring a large saucepan of salted water to the boil. Cook the asparagus until just tender, about 2 minutes. Remove with a slotted spoon and keep warm. Add the leeks and simmer until al dente, 2–3 minutes. Drain and keep warm.

6 Remove the fillets from the saddles and slice on an angle. Arrange each fillet on a serving plate in a fan. Build a lattice of five asparagus spears and five leeks per plate behind the rabbit, and drizzle with sauce. To serve, garnish with the strips of belly flap.

Curtis Stone

Rabbit with chickpeas, rosemary, garlic, and preserved lemon

Rabbits, once the scourge of Australia, and hapless speed humps on country roads, now enjoy a place of pride in my repertoire. I love cooking rabbit: the meat has a subtle flavour, and a wonderful tender texture — and it's cheap. This recipe uses big flavours to lift the subtlety of the rabbit, and it's simple to do. Rabbit is ideal with steamed spinach or creamy mashed potatoes.

SERVES 4

2	rabbits, weighing about 3 lb (1.5 kg)*	2
3½ oz	seasoned all-purpose flour	100 g
⅓ cup	olive oil	75 mL
20	cloves garlic, peeled	20
½ cup	fresh rosemary leaves	125 mL
1¼ cups	dry white wine	300 mL
4 cups	chicken stock	1 L
7 oz	drained canned chickpeas	200 g
2	preserved lemon rind quarters, sliced**	2
	Salt and freshly ground black pepper	

1 Dredge the rabbit joints in the seasoned flour. Shake off the excess. Heat 3 tbsp (45 mL) oil in a large heavy-based flameproof pot or Dutch oven and fry the rabbit, in batches, until golden brown. Remove from the pan. Drain off excess oil and wipe out the burnt flour with paper towels.

2 Preheat the oven to 350°F (180°C). Re-heat the pot and add the remaining oil. Replace the rabbit joints. Add the garlic and rosemary, and fry for a minute or 2 to develop the flavours. Add the wine, stock, chickpeas and preserved lemon. Bring to a simmer and cover with waxed paper, then the lid.

3 Transfer to the oven, and bake for 40 minutes. To check that the rabbit is cooked, press the flesh with your fingers; it should give way under pressure. Remove the rabbit from the pot. Reduce the cooking juices over a moderately high heat until they coat the back of a spoon. Season to taste with salt and pepper. Return the rabbit to the pot, reheat and serve.

* Ask your butcher to joint the rabbits into legs, shoulders and two saddle cuts.
** Jars of preserved lemon can be found in delicatessens and large supermarkets.

Grilled T-bone steak with garlic and anchovy butter

I have always loved cooking meat on the bone. The meat keeps a certain kind of sweetness, and lends itself to a relaxed style of eating — or perhaps it's just me who loves gnawing on the bone. I also find that anchovies work particularly well with hearty meats, such as beef or lamb.

SERVES 4

1 cup	unsalted butter, softened	250 mL
2	cloves garlic, minced	2
3	lightly salted anchovy fillets, finely chopped	3
1	large shallot, finely chopped	1
2 tbsp	finely chopped fresh flat-leaf parsley	30 mL
	Salt and freshly ground black pepper	
4	T-bone steaks, weighing about 1 lb (500 g)	4
1 tbsp	olive oil	15 mL
5	large field mushrooms, thickly sliced	5
¼ cup	Worcestershire sauce	50 mL
4	anchovy fillets, halved lengthways, to garnish	4

1. Place the butter, garlic, anchovies, shallot, and parsley in a large bowl, and season with salt and pepper. Beat together until smooth. Take a large sheet of plastic wrap and spoon the butter in a rough log shape towards one end. Roll up the butter, pressing it into a firm, thick sausage as you go. Roll the sausage on the bench to give a smooth surface, then transfer to the refrigerator to harden.

2. Brush the steaks with the oil. Fry in a hot skillet over moderately high heat for 2–3 minutes on each side, or to your liking. Cut off 4 discs of butter and place 1 on top of each steak. Remove the skillet from the heat and rest the steak for 3–4 minutes in a warm place before serving.

3. Meanwhile, heat another skillet until very hot. Add the mushrooms and Worcestershire sauce, and stir to deglaze for 1–2 minutes. Stack the mushrooms in the centre of 4 serving plates and place a T-bone on top of each pile. Place 2 anchovy strips in a cross on the steaks, and serve.

Note: Any unused butter will keep in the refrigerator for up to 10 days, or in the freezer for 3 months.

Curtis Stone

Citrus and honey almond cake

It was great to hear Curtis's mum telling stories of how he used to love sucking on their local honeycomb when he was a kid, so I thought that in tribute to the big sucker I'd make a suitable cake in his honour.

SERVES 8

7 fl oz	honey	200 mL
1 cup	unsalted butter, softened	250 mL
3	free-range eggs	3
1 lb	ground almonds	500 g
1 tsp	baking powder	5 mL
	Finely grated rind and juice of 1 medium orange	
	Finely grated rind and juice of 1 lemon	
	Finely grated rind and juice of 1 lime	
	Icing sugar for dusting	

1 Preheat the oven to 300°F (150°C). Grease a 10-inch (3-L) springform pan and line with waxed paper. Warm the honey in hot water or in a microwave oven. Place in a large bowl, add the butter, and beat until thoroughly combined. Add the eggs, one at a time, beating well after each addition.

2 Stir in the ground almonds and baking powder. Add the orange, lemon and lime rind and juice, and mix until evenly combined. Pour the mixture into the prepared pan. Bake in the oven for 1 1/2 hours, or until a small knife inserted into the centre comes out clean. Place on a wire rack, and cool completely in the pan. Turn out and dust with icing sugar.

Ben O'Donoghue

Rhubarb tarte fine with honey and cinnamon ice cream

My mum grows rhubarb in her garden, so I have always had a soft spot for it. I think it has a lovely tart taste that is perfectly matched with something sweet and a little spicy — the honey and cinnamon ice cream is the perfect complement. Alternatively, buy some good-quality vanilla ice cream and soften it a little. Mix some ground cinnamon and honey into it and serve.

SERVES 4

7 oz	block puff pastry	200 g
6	rhubarb stalks, very finely sliced on the diagonal	6

1. Preheat the oven to 400°F (200°C), and line a baking sheet with waxed paper. On a lightly floured surface, roll out the puff pastry to a thickness of about 1/4 inch (5 mm). Cut out a neat circle 8 inches (20 cm) in diameter and transfer to the prepared baking sheet.

2. Using a sharp knife, make even cuts 1/4-inch (5-mm) long right around the perimeter of the pastry. Fill the tart by arranging the rhubarb slices on top in a circular pattern. Place a piece of waxed paper over the tart, followed by a second baking sheet to weigh down the rhubarb. Transfer to the oven and bake for 25–30 minutes, or until the pastry is golden (it doesn't puff because of the weight) and the rhubarb cooked. Cut into quarters and serve each with a scoop of Honey and Cinnamon Ice cream.

continued over...

Curtis Stone

Honey and cinnamon ice cream

SERVES 6–8

7 fl oz	18% cream	200 mL
1¼ cups	milk	300 mL
1½ tbsp	instant dissolving sugar	
1 tsp	ground cinnamon	
1	vanilla bean, split in half lengthways	1
½ tsp	freshly grated nutmeg	2 mL
1	whole clove, crushed	1
7	free-range egg yolks	7
½ cup	honey	125 mL

1 Put the cream and 1 cup (250 mL) milk in a large saucepan. Add the sugar, cinnamon, vanilla, nutmeg, and clove. Place over moderate heat, and bring to just below boiling point.

2 In a bowl, beat the remaining milk with the egg yolks and honey until smooth. Add the milk mixture, whisking constantly. Pour everything back into the saucepan and return to the heat. Cook over low heat, whisking constantly, until slightly thickened. Strain into a shallow bowl and chill.

3 Once cold, transfer the mixture to an ice-cream machine and churn until semi set. Remove and freeze.

Curtis Stone

Byron Bay

Byron Bay

Beaches, Nuts, and Babes

Ben O'Donoghue

Byron Bay, with its epic beaches of crystal-clear water, and amazing views of Mount Warning and the rolling hills of the hinterland, is one of the centres of Australia's counter-culture. Hippies, ferals, surfers, organic farmers, and tourists flock to this naturally beautiful region where the rainforest meets the sea. It's a zoo!

Cape Byron is the most easterly point of Australia, and the lighthouse on the headland is a famous landmark. Byron is also famous as a place for whale watching during the season from June to September — ironically, because whaling was one of Australia's first industries, and a whaling station operated at Byron Bay until 1962.

I first went to Byron Bay with a bunch of mates on the way back from a music festival in Brisbane; it was all a bit of a blur. The next time I went was to meet Peter, my girlfriend's father, so I was a little better behaved.

The reason we were there this time was simple. My partner De-arne was returning to Byron Bay to see her dad, and to join up with Curtis and me. With her was our twelve-week-old beautiful baby, Ruby. Curtis and I had planned this food discovery trip for a long time, and when Dee and I knew we were going to have a baby, it was she who insisted we carry our plans through. No wonder I love her so much.

I had been with Dee in London for Ruby's birth and her first month. When it was time to leave, I couldn't believe how difficult it was. I couldn't let go at the airport, and thought of them, over and over, every day. Just before I left London I got one of those right-trendy mobile phones that can receive photos, and almost every day Dee had been emailing me a new pic of Ruby so that I could feel connected. In the short time I'd been away, Ruby had discovered her vocal

Coolangatta
Tweed Heads

Murwillumbah ●

Mount Warning ▲

Mullumbimby ● ● Brunswick Heads

Kyogle ●

● Nimbin

Peppers Resort ■

Cape Byron

St Helena ■ ● Byron Bay

Bangalow ● *Brookfarm*

Zendvelds Coffee ■

Lismore ●

cords. Dee would put her on the phone to 'Arrh' and 'Oooh', and tug at my heartstrings. Curtis always knew when I'd been talking to them as I think I must have looked a little misty.

Curtis and I flew into Coolangatta airport. The flight seemed to take forever. At the airport we found Dee and a sleeping Ruby waiting. I couldn't stop looking at Ruby, even though she didn't wake up once. I hoped she was like that every night …

We were planning to cater for a casual family get-together to celebrate Ruby's birth. That meant Curtis and I needed to jump into a car, and find some fresh local produce. Oh, and if it was nap time for Ruby, maybe we could squeeze in a surf or two in one of the most beautiful locations in the country.

Bright and early in the morning, Curtis banged on my door, stumbling in from a big night out. He had noticed that one of the trawlers at Brunswick Heads, just up the coast, had come in, and suggested we jump in the car, and go down and see what they had. That boy's got stamina!

Brunswick Heads is an idyllic seaside village where fishing boats and trawlers are protected by a natural harbour. We got there just as they'd finished unloading. There were some good-sized eastern tiger shrimp and Ted and Bruce, the fishermen, reckoned we were lucky because there had been a full moon, which usually makes catching shrimp virtually impossible. Apparently, during the full moon shrimp are easily seen by all kinds of hungry predators, and so spend their time hidden under rocks, ledges, and in groves of sea grass. There was a good catch of octopus, too, and as I know that Pete loves squid and octopus, I took some just for him.

We decided to look for more produce at the local Byron Bay Saturday Markets. It's a farmer's-direct market and most of the producers there are small time and organic, which means that the produce is sensational. We found exotic fruit, nuts, herbs, chutneys, sauces, wheat grass, and eggs, and met Kay of Byron Sauces, from whom we got the most amazing lime dressing.

We also met Hugh, who farms free-range eggs. His family lives on one of the original Byron Bay cattle properties. He loves chooks, and his mates call his place the 'Henhouse Hilton.' Better still, he's a surfer, so we made a date to catch up later that day. Hugh took us to some great out-of-the-way local breaks — when it comes to surfing, local knowledge is gold. The waves were wicked — small but great — and beautiful to surf.

I had decided to do a pork dish, as Dee's dad loves pork. Hugh suggested we take a drive to Bangalow, and visit John the butcher. It's bloody beautiful once you get into the Byron Bay hinterland. It's a mix of rainforest and lush farmland. And it's green, every shade of green you can imagine.

Driving to Bangalow we were diverted by a small sign directing us to Brookfarm in St Helena. Here Pamela and Martin Brook grow macadamia nuts. They have 4500 trees snaking in row after row over the hills, and into the valleys of their property. They don't just grow for nuts but for macadamia oil. The nuts are allowed to ripen on the tree, and drop naturally to the ground. That's when they are harvested. Macadamias are native Australian rainforest trees, and all the original plants that are now farmed around the world originally came from Australia.

Bangalow is a nice little town, and the main street looks like it's out of a Ned Kelly movie set with its original heritage buildings dotting the main strip. At the butcher's shop we met the larger-than-life John Herane. John's is an old-fashioned butcher's shop with heaps of advice dispensed with every cut.

Last call was to the Zendvelds' coffee plantation. We were surprised to learn that coffee was grown in the Byron region — but it has been, since the 1880s. The Zendvelds have 20,000 trees under cultivation, which, by world standards is small, but they concentrate only on Arabica beans. Rebecca Zendveld showed us the trellised vines with beans ready for picking. They are bright red — it's no wonder they are called cherries. After picking, this red husk is removed because it's the bean, or seed, at the centre we're after. Even at this stage the bean doesn't look like what we know as coffee — it's a kind of beige colour, and looks more like an overgrown lentil.

Then Rebecca took us into her dark domain — the roasting shed. She is the blender and roaster, and one of the few 'roast mistresses' in Australia. Roasting turns a simple bean into useable coffee. The roaster is to coffee as the winemaker and blender is to wine. When the roaster (the machine) is fired to the correct temperature, in go the raw beans. After that, there's a constant process of checking until the beans reach the colour Rebecca is looking for. The aroma in the shed is amazing. The beans are tumbled out of the roaster, and onto a flat resting area where cool air is forced from below to stop them cooking. The coffee they make here is naturally low in caffeine. Apparently, low-quality soils produce high caffeine, as caffeine is nature's defense against pests. But here in the Byron highlands where volcanic soils are rich, and pests few and far between, the coffee bushes don't need to make as much caffeine.

Once we'd found the pork, shrimp and all the other accompaniments, Curtis and I headed to Peppers Resort in the rainforest where the family gathering had been arranged. A barbecue had been placed on the wide deck overlooking the natural rainforest valley. Curtis was a great help, and we got stuck into preparing the food. Once the entire family had arrived, we fired up the barbie, and got the show on the road. It was great fun with great food, and great company. A fantastic way to end our short visit back in Oz.

Barbecued sweet corn with lime, chilli, and Parmesan butter

The first time I tasted these flavours I was in New York at a little Cuban café on Prince Street, and thought wow! Now this recipe is a regular number on my barbecue menu at home. It's so simple to prepare, and great fun to eat.

SERVES 4

4	corn cobs, in their husks	4
3¹/₂ fl oz	unsalted butter, softened	100 mL
3¹/₂ oz	Parmesan cheese, freshly grated	100 g
	Finely grated rind of 2 large limes	
1–2	bird's-eye chilies, seeded and finely chopped	1–2
	Salt and freshly ground black pepper	
1	lime, quartered	1

1 Preheat the barbecue or grill to high. Place the corn cobs on the barbecue or grill and cook for 15 minutes, turning often, until golden brown. Peel off the husks when cool enough to handle.

2 While the corn is cooking, combine the butter, Parmesan, rind and chili in a bowl, and beat until smooth. Season with salt and pepper. Smear each cob with the butter mixture and serve with a wedge of lime.

Ben O'Donoghue

Baby spinach and feta salad

This is your basic Greek salad, but better. It involves a little more work but, boy, the flavours — and it goes really well with Pete's octopus (page 238).

SERVES 4

1	large red onion, thinly sliced	1
2	Lebanese cucumbers (any cucumber will do), thinly sliced	2
4 tsp	instant dissolving sugar	20 mL
1 tbsp	sea salt	15 mL
1/4 cup	white wine vinegar	50 mL
1/4 cup	finely chopped fresh dillweed	50 mL
7 oz	good-quality feta cheese	200 g
4 cups	loosely packed baby spinach leaves	1 L
1 tbsp	aged balsamic vinegar	15 mL
1 tbsp	extra-virgin olive oil	15 mL
2 oz	pine nuts, toasted	60 g

1. Place the onion and cucumber in a glass bowl. Add the sugar, salt, white wine vinegar and 1 tbsp (15 mL) dillweed. Leave for 30 minutes.

2. Break the feta into chunks and toss with the spinach and the remaining dillweed. Drain the onion and cucumber mixture and add to the feta. Add the balsamic vinegar and oil, and gently toss to coat well. Sprinkle with the pine nuts to serve.

Ben O'Donoghue

Chinese-style combination soup

This soup is in the same family as the famous chicken, sweet corn and shark's fin soup. Basically, if you start off with a good base (stock) you can't go wrong. If you don't like any of the listed ingredients, then replace them with ones you do like. The soup is just so adaptable — if you prefer seafood, use fish stock and substitute the chicken and pork for crab and squid.

SERVES 6–8

8 cups	chicken stock	2 L
1	boneless, skinless chicken breast, weighing about 8 oz (250 g)	1
1	pork fillet, weighing about 8 oz (250 g)	1
4	green king shrimp, peeled and deveined	4
1	carrot, thinly sliced	1
4	baby corn cobs, thinly sliced	4
3^1/$_2$ oz	bamboo shoots, thinly sliced	100 g
^{1}/$_3$ cup	cornflour	75 mL
^{1}/$_3$ cup	water	75 mL
2	free-range eggs	2
1	bird's-eye chili, finely chopped	1
8	green onions, thinly sliced	8
	Light soy sauce to taste	
	Fish sauce to taste	
	Sesame oil to taste	

1. Pour the stock into a large saucepan and bring to just below boiling. Add the chicken and pork, and poach for 2–3 minutes. Remove and cool for 10 minutes. Shred, then return to the stock.

2. Slice each shrimp into 6 pieces. Add to the stock along with the carrot, corn, and bamboo shoots. Bring to the boil. Blend the cornflour with the water to form a paste, and slowly stir into the soup. Return to the boil, reduce heat to low, and simmer until thickened.

3. Crack the eggs into a small bowl and lightly beat with a fork. Remove the soup from the heat. While stirring in a circular motion, slowly add the eggs in a thin stream, creating egg flowers. Add the chili and green onion, and season to taste with light soy sauce, fish sauce, and sesame oil.

Curtis Stone

Pete's octopus

In terms of food, Byron once meant avocados, macadamia nuts and magic mushrooms. Now it's all gourmet delicatessens, modern restaurants and grower's markets. Pete, my girlfriend's old man, loves octopus, so I thought that while I was in Byron Bay I had to dedicate a dish to him. He loves baby octopus, but I like the larger stuff; you can't have everything, mate. The best octopus to buy is the double-sucker variety (the suckers are usually side-by-side along the leg); I don't know why, but they just cook up better. This recipe involves cooking the occy twice. It can be served with aioli, or any other dip you like, or with a Greek salad.

SERVES 4–6

4 lb	double-sucker octopus	2 kg
1	clove garlic, minced	1
2 tbsp	finely chopped fresh flat-leaf parsley	30 mL
1 tbsp	finely chopped fresh thyme leaves	15 mL
1	dried red chili, crumbled	1
	Juice of 1 lemon	
2 tbsp	olive oil	30 mL

1. Preheat the oven to 250°F (120°C), and place a wire rack over a roasting pan. Cut the head off the octopus and discard. Rinse the body under running water, remove the beak, then split the body in half to give two pieces with four tentacles each. Spread out on the wire rack and place in the oven. Roast for 2$1/2$–3 hours, until the flesh is shrivelled and dry around the edges, but tender enough to push your fingers through. Trim off the suckers and any overly dry bits.

2. Slice the tentacles into finger-size pieces. Combine the garlic, parsley, thyme, and chili in a bowl, and toss through the octopus. Add the lemon juice and oil and leave for 30 minutes. Preheat the barbecue to high. Place on the hot barbecue plate and grill until browned. Serve immediately.

Ben O'Donoghue

Salt and pepper shrimp with an aromatic salad

The first time I ate salt and pepper squid, I was impressed with its simplicity. I went back to my kitchen and fiddled around with other seafood and found that shrimp also work really well. Shrimp cook very quickly, so try not to have them in the hot oil for more than a minute.

SERVES 4

12	green king shrimp	12
1/2 cup	cornflour	125 mL
2 tbsp	sea salt	30 mL
1 tsp	freshly ground black pepper	5 mL
Pinch	dried hot pepper flakes	
2	free-range eggs, lightly beaten	2
	Peanut oil for deep-frying	
4 tsp	olive oil	20 mL
1 tbsp	lime juice	15 mL
	Salt and freshly ground black pepper	
6 cups	loosely packed mixed salad and herb leaves (coriander, dillweed, basil, watercress, oak leaf lettuce, wild arugula)	1.5 L
1 1/2 lb	red and yellow cherry tomatoes, quartered	750 g

1 Peel and devein the shrimp, leaving the head and tail intact. Combine the cornflour, salt, pepper and pepper flakes in a bowl. Toss the shrimp in the seasoned cornflour, dip in the eggs, then coat with the cornflour again.

2 Place enough peanut oil in a work or deep skillet to come halfway up the pan. Fry the shrimp, 3 or 4 at a time, until golden. Drain on paper towels. Whisk the olive oil and lime juice together, and season to taste with salt and pepper. Toss through the salad leaves and tomato quarters. Pile the salad leaves in the centre of 4 serving plates and arrange the shrimp around the salad.

Curtis Stone

King shrimp, haloumi, and pineapple skewers with lime, chilli, and mint salsa

SERVES 4

12	long thick rosemary stalks or bamboo skewers	12

Salsa

5	large red chilies, pricked with a fork	5
	Finely grated rind and juice of 1 lime	
1 tsp	sugar	5 mL
1/3 cup	peanut or corn oil	75 mL
1 tbsp	finely chopped fresh mint leaves	15 mL
1	vine-ripened tomato, peeled, seeded and finely chopped	1
12	green king shrimp, peeled and deveined	12
1	pineapple, peeled and chopped into bite-size chunks	1
8 oz	haloumi cheese, chopped into bite-size chunks	250 g

1 Strip the leaves from the rosemary stalks, keeping a tuft at the top. Soak stalks or skewers in cold water for 30 minutes to prevent them from burning on the barbecue. Preheat the barbecue to high.

2 To make the salsa, cook the chilies on the barbecue until charred. Place in a small bowl and cover with plastic wrap. When cool, remove the skin and seeds and tear the flesh into strips. Place in a clean bowl and toss with the lime rind and juice, sugar, oil, mint, and tomato.

3 Thread a shrimp, a piece of pineapple and a piece of haloumi onto each skewer. Repeat once more, finishing each skewer with a shrimp.

4 Grill on the barbecue until the shrimp are cooked through and the pineapple and haloumi are slightly charred, 5–8 minutes. Serve with a liberal drizzle of salsa.

Ben O'Donoghue

Caramelized spinach gnocchi and quattro formaggio

Gnocchi is one of those dishes that if it is done well, is fantastic. In this particular dish the gnocchi is pre-cooked and chilled, then just before serving, it is pan-fried. This makes the gnocchi crisp on the outside and nice and soft on the inside.

SERVES 4–6

1 lb	floury potatoes, russet are good, unpeeled	500 g
3 cups	tightly packed baby spinach leaves	750 mL
4 oz	pasta (00 Italian) flour plus extra	125 g
1	large free-range egg yolk	1
	Freshly grated nutmeg to taste	
	Salt and freshly ground black pepper	

Sauce

1 cup	milk	250 mL
²/₃ cup	18% cream	150 mL
1¹/₂ oz	Taleggio cheese	45 g
1¹/₂ oz	gorgonzola cheese	45 g
1¹/₂ oz	mascarpone cheese	45 g
¹/₄ cup	freshly grated Parmesan cheese	50 mL
1 tbsp	finely chopped fresh flat-leaf parsley	15 mL
	Salt and freshly ground black pepper	
4 cups	tightly packed spinach leaves	1 L
	Shaved Parmesan cheese to garnish	

1. Preheat the oven to 350°F (180°C). Place the potatoes on a roasting pan and roast in the oven for 1¹/₄–1¹/₂ hours, depending on size, until tender. Cool for 10 minutes. Halve and scoop out the flesh. While still warm, pass through a ricer or mouli. Do not use a food processor, as this will pulp the potatoes and draw out the starch. Cover and allow to cool.

2. Rinse the spinach and shake dry. Place in a large, hot saucepan and heat, tossing often, until wilted. Remove and chop finely. Transfer to a clean dry tea towel and squeeze out all the liquid.

3. Gently combine the potatoes, spinach, flour and egg yolk, and knead lightly for 15–20 seconds. You want a soft, lightly worked dough, so add extra flour only if the dough sticks to your hands. Season lightly with nutmeg, salt and pepper. Divide into three or four manageable portions and roll each into a small log about the size of a breakfast sausage. Using a sharp knife, cut each log into 1¹/₄-inch (3-cm) lengths. Indent one side of the gnocchi with the tines of a fork. Place them in a single layer on a tray, and transfer to the refrigerator.

continued over...

Curtis Stone

④ Bring a large saucepan of salted water to the boil. Cook the gnocchi in batches for 1–1¹/₂ minutes, until they float to the surface. Remove gnocchi and plunge into ice water. Once cool, pat dry with paper towels. In a hot, non-stick skillet, cook gnocchi for about 1 minute on each side, until caramelized, or golden.

⑤ To make the sauce, slowly bring the milk and cream to the boil. Add the four cheeses, reduce the heat to low and simmer, stirring constantly, until the cheeses melt. Purée, then pass through a sieve into a clean saucepan. Reheat, then add the parsley, and salt and pepper to taste.

⑥ Wilt the additional spinach in a hot saucepan, tossing frequently. Remove and chop finely. Squeeze out all liquid using a clean dry tea towel. Reheat in a little sauce.

⑦ To serve, place the spinach in the centre of the serving bowls. Spoon in equal quantities of the sauce, then divide the gnocchi among the bowls, arranging around the spinach. Garnish the spinach with shaved Parmesan.

Curtis Stone

Escalopes of pork with fava bean salad

This is another great summer recipe. Char-grilling pork gives it such a lovely flavour and with this lively salad the flavours are bright and light. I can just imagine the cool early evening breeze, with a nice chilled Sauvignon Blanc and the fresh flavours of this salad. Get your butcher to bash out four 1-inch (2.5 cm) thick cuts of pork loin which have a little fat left on the meat.

SERVES 4

Dry marinade

1 tbsp	finely chopped fresh thyme leaves	15 mL
2	cloves garlic, finely chopped	2
	Finely grated rind of 2 lemons	
1/2 tsp	freshly ground black pepper	2 mL
1/2 tsp	dried lemon myrtle leaves*	2 mL

4 pork escalopes, as above

Salad

2 lb	unshelled fresh young fava beans**	1 kg
5 oz	canned lima beans, drained	150 g
1	medium red onion, finely chopped	1
1 1/2 cups	loosely packed fresh basil leaves, roughly torn	375 mL
2 tbsp	chopped fresh flat-leaf parsley	30 mL

Dressing

2 tbsp	olive oil	30 mL
	Juice of 2 lemons	
	Salt and freshly ground black pepper	
4 cups	loosely packed wild arugula	1 L

1. To make the dry marinade, combine the thyme, garlic, rind, black pepper, and lemon myrtle. Sprinkle over the pork and leave to stand for 15 minutes.

2. To make the salad, shell the fava beans. Combine with the lima beans, onion, basil and parsley.

3. To make the dressing, whisk olive oil with half the lemon juice, and season to taste with salt and pepper. Pour half over the salad and toss lightly. Pour the remaining half over the arugula leaves and toss to coat.

4. Preheat the barbecue to high. Brush the hot barbecue plate with a little olive oil and grill the pork, about 1 minute per side. Remove from the barbecue and squeeze with the remaining lemon juice.

5. Pile the fava bean salad in the centre of 4 serving plates. Top with an escalope of pork, then scatter the arugula over the top.

* If lemon myrtle is not available try using 1 teaspoon of thinly sliced fresh lemongrass as a substitute.
** Where fresh young fava beans are unavailable, use 1 lb (500 g) of shelled larger beans or frozen beans. Both will need to be blanched for 1 minute, then shelled.

Ben O'Donoghue

Chocolate and espresso pudding

I do this dessert in my restaurant in London where it just flies out the door. Coffee is one of those flavours that goes well with chocolate. I like to use espresso coffee, but not everyone has an espresso machine, so use good-quality instant coffee granules instead.

SERVES 6

Ice-cubes

2 oz	milk chocolate, chopped	60 g
1/4 cup	hot and very strong espresso coffee	50 mL

Batter

8 oz	dark chocolate (70% cocoa solids), chopped	250 g
1 cup	cold butter, cubed	250 mL
8	free-range egg yolks	8
4 tbsp	rice flour	60 mL
4	free-range egg whites	4
	Instant dissolving sugar for dusting	
	Icing sugar for dusting	

1 To make the ice-cubes, combine the milk chocolate and hot coffee in a bowl, and stir until chocolate is melted and smooth. Pour into 6 ice-cube moulds, and freeze until set, about 3 hours.

2 To make the batter, gently melt the chocolate and butter in a heavy-based saucepan, stirring until smooth. Beat the egg yolks in a large bowl until light and fluffy, then fold into the chocolate mixture. Sift the rice flour into the bowl, and stir to combine. In a separate bowl, whisk the egg whites until soft peaks form, and fold into the chocolate mixture. If necessary, the batter will keep for several hours.

3 Preheat the oven to 350°F (180°C) and place a baking sheet on the centre shelf. Butter six 2/3-cup (150-mL) cappuccino cups or ovenproof custard cups, and dust with the instant dissolving sugar. Spoon enough batter into the cups to fill by one-third. Place an ice-cube in the centre, then cover with the remaining batter.

continued over...

4. Transfer the cups to the baking sheet in the oven, and bake for 15–18 minutes. Turn the heat off and open the oven door. Leave the puddings to rest for 2 minutes.

5. To serve, gently run the tip of a knife around the edge of the puddings, turn out onto a plate, and dust with icing sugar. The outside should be the texture of a light sponge, with the centre runny. If you have difficulty in removing the pudding, just dust it with icing sugar and serve it in the cup.

Ben O'Donoghue

Chocolate fondant

The word fondant translates as melt. When you break into the pudding, the centre of it melts all over the plate. It's a bit like a self-saucing pudding — very indulgent, not something you eat every day, but if you decide to indulge, I promise you will be a repeat offender.

SERVES 4

	Unsweetened cocoa powder for dusting	
7 oz	dark chocolate (70% cocoa solids), chopped	200 g
7 oz	butter	200 g
4	free-range eggs	4
4	free-range egg yolks	4
3½ oz	sugar	100 g
½ cup	all-purpose flour	125 mL

Sauce

1 cup	18% cream	250 mL
8 oz	dark chocolate (70% cocoa solids), chopped	250 g

Good-quality vanilla ice cream to serve

1 Preheat the oven to 400°F (200°C). Grease four 3-inch (125-mL) dariole moulds or four ½-cup (125-mL) ovenproof custard cups, and dust with sifted cocoa.

2 Melt the chocolate and butter in a heavy-based saucepan over a low heat, stirring until smooth. Whisk the eggs, egg yolks and sugar until pale and doubled in volume, about 3–4 minutes. Fold in the melted chocolate mixture. Add the flour, and whisk until smooth. Pour into the prepared moulds and bake for 12–16 minutes, until just set. Rest for 3–4 minutes.

3 To make the sauce, bring the cream to just below boiling point in a heavy-based saucepan. Turn off the heat, and add the chocolate. Stir constantly until melted and smooth.

4 To serve, run a sharp knife around the inside wall of each mould to loosen the fondant. Invert each mould over a serving plate and, holding the two together, give a sharp little shake to loosen. The fondant will slide out onto the plate. Serve with vanilla ice cream and the chocolate sauce spooned over the top.

Curtis Stone

Pear and macadamia nut crumble

Macadamia nuts, like most nuts, have a high fat content. That is why they give a lovely richness to puddings and desserts, as well as being great in savoury dishes. Crumbles can be made out of a lot of different fruits, anything from pears to rhubarb to stone fruits.

SERVES 4–6

8	Bartlett pears, peeled, cored and quartered	8
3¹/₂ oz	instant dissolving sugar	100 g
	Finely grated rind and juice of 1 orange	
1	cinnamon stick	1
1	vanilla bean, split in half lengthways	1

Crumble

10 oz	all-purpose flour	300 g
¹/₂ cup	instant dissolving sugar	125 mL
3¹/₂ oz	toasted and crushed macadamia nuts	100 g
¹/₂ cup	butter, softened	125 mL

Good-quality vanilla ice cream to serve

1 Preheat the oven to 325°F (160°C), and grease a 6-cup (1.5 L) ovenproof dish.

2 Place the pears in a medium saucepan with the sugar, rind and juice, cinnamon, and vanilla. Cover, and cook over medium heat for about 20 minutes, depending on the ripeness of the pears, until the pears are tender, but not mushy. Remove the cinnamon and vanilla. Spoon the pears into the prepared dish.

3 To make the crumble, combine the flour, sugar and macadamia nuts in a bowl. Add the butter, and using your fingers, rub it into the mixture until evenly distributed. Scatter over the pears and transfer the dish to the oven. Bake for 15–20 minutes, until golden brown on top. Serve warm, with vanilla ice cream.

Curtis Stone

Index